OXFORD BIBLE SERIES

General Editors
P. R. Ackroyd and G. N. Stanton

OXFORD BIBLE SERIES

General Editors
P. R. Ackroyd and G. N. Stanton

Introducing the Old Testament   Richard J. Coggins
Narrative in the Hebrew Bible   David M. Gunn and
Danna Fewell
forthcoming
Psalmody and Poetry in the Old Testament   Sue Gillingham
forthcoming
Prophecy and the Prophets of the Old Testament
John F. A. Sawyer

Wisdom and Law in the Old Testament. The Ordering of
Life in Israel and Early Judaism   J. Blenkinsopp

The Origins of Christianity: A Historical Introduction to
the New Testament   Schuyler Brown

The Gospels and Jesus   Graham N. Stanton

Variety and Unity in New Testament Thought   J. Reumann
forthcoming
Pauline Christianity   John Ziesler
revised edition
Biblical Interpretation   Robert Morgan with John Barton

Pauline Christianity

J. A. ZIESLER

Revised Edition

Oxford   New York
OXFORD UNIVERSITY PRESS

Oxford University Press, Walton Street, Oxford OX2 6DP
Oxford New York Toronto
Delhi Bombay Calcutta Madras Karachi
Kuala Lumpur Singapore Hong Kong Tokyo
Nairobi Dar es Salaam Cape Town
Melbourne Auckland Madrid
and associated companies in
Berlin Ibadan

Oxford is a trade mark of Oxford University Press

Published in the United States by
Oxford University Press Inc., New York

© J. A. Ziesler 1983

Revised edition 1990

British Library Cataloguing in Publication Data
Data available

Library of Congress Cataloging in Publication Data
Ziesler, J. A.
Pauline Christianity. (Oxford Bible series)
1. Bible. N.T. Epistles of Paul—Theology.
2. Paul, the Apostle. Saint—Influence. 3. Church
history—Primitive and early church, ca. 30–600.
I. Title. II. Series.
BS2651.Z53 1983 227'.6 82–19022
ISBN 0–19–826460–7
ISBN 0–19–826459–3 (pbk)

5 7 9 10 8 6 4

Printed in Great Britain on acid-free paper by
Biddles Ltd., Guildford and King's Lynn

GENERAL EDITORS' PREFACE

There are many commentaries on individual books of the Bible, but the reader who wishes to take a broader view has less choice. This series is intended to meet this need. Its structure is thematic, with each volume embracing a number of biblical books. It is designed for use with any of the familiar translations of the Bible; quotations are normally from RSV, but the authors of the individual volumes also use other translations or make their own where this helps to bring out the particular meaning of a passage.

To provide general orientation, there are two volumes of a more introductory character: one will consider the Old Testament in its cultural and historical context, the other the New Testament, discussing the origins of Christianity. Four volumes deal with different kinds of material in the Old Testament: narrative, prophecy, poetry/psalmody, wisdom and law. Three volumes handle different aspects of the New Testament: the Gospels, Paul and Pauline Christianity, the varieties of New Testament thought. One volume looks at the nature of biblical interpretation, covering both Testaments.

The authors of the individual volumes write for a general readership. Technical terms and Hebrew or Greek words are explained; the latter are used only when essential to the understanding of the text. The general introductory volumes are designed to stand on their own, providing a framework, but also to serve to raise some of the questions which the remaining volumes examine in closer detail. All the volumes other than the two general ones include discussion of selected biblical passages in greater depth, thus providing examples of the ways in which the interpretation of the text makes possible deeper understanding of the wider issues, both historical and theological, with which the Bible is concerned. Select bibliographies in each volume point the way to further discussion of the many issues which remain open to fuller exploration.

P.R.A.
G.N.S.

NOTE

CONTENTS

KEY PASSAGES DISCUSSED

1

Introduction

Pauline Christianity is the earliest for which we have direct documentary evidence. Despite the arrangement of books in the New Testament, the earliest gospel was written after the latest of Paul's letters, and it is Paul who lets us into the ground floor of the early church. A church receiving a letter from him probably had no other Christian writing, and as it was far removed from Palestine and from the memories of the followers of Jesus, it probably knew little of the oral tradition of his deeds and words. It had, of course, heard the preaching of Paul or someone else, and it may have had access to the Septuagint (the Greek translation of the Jewish Scriptures), but we cannot assume any more than this. In large areas of the Christian world Paul's gospel was the only one people had heard at first, and the idea that Paul complicated an originally simple gospel of Jesus simply does not fit; in many places it would be decades before a written gospel circulated. Of course there was earlier Christianity in Palestine, but all our documentary evidence for it is later than the undisputed letters of Paul.

The earliest Pauline letter is probably 1 Thessalonians, about AD 50–51, or twenty years after the crucifixion, though it could be even earlier. Paul nowhere says how long after the ministry of Jesus he became a Christian, but it was about the middle thirties: he had to escape from Damascus when Aretas was king of Nabataea (2 Cor. 11: 32f.) and this is probably Aretas IV, who controlled Damascus from 37 to 39. So, whether the crucifixion was in 30 or 33, Paul appears as an active follower of Christ less than a decade later. There is thus no doubt that he is a very early witness to Christianity.

An apostle

Paul is usually depicted as one whose zeal for the Jewish Law made him persecute Christians because they were being lax about it and encouraging others to be lax as well. While on his way to Damascus to pursue his crusade against them, he encountered Christ in a remarkable vision. He was not only converted but called to be the apostle to the Gentiles. After instruction by other Christians, and a time for thought and preparation, he began his missionary work, first in Syrian Antioch but then in three great journeys going ever farther west. After many tribulations he was eventually nearly lynched in the Temple at Jerusalem, but his arrest by the Romans saved him. He appealed as a Roman citizen to be tried by Caesar in Rome, fearing the influence of the Jewish authorities in Jerusalem over the local magistrates. He died in Rome after a period in prison during Nero's persecution, about the year 65. It was because he was lax about the Jewish Law and encouraged others to be lax that he incurred so much hostility from those whose zeal was very much what his own had once been.

The above picture derives partly from tradition, partly from the letters, and partly from the Acts of the Apostles. It will serve as a rough outline, though several details in it are inaccurate: he himself did not call his encounter a vision, and it ought not to be called a conversion but a commissioning, and 'three missionary journeys' is a misleading description of his work. He did not set out on missionary expeditions and return periodically for home leave, and there is no evidence that he saw any particular place as his headquarters or his journeyings as having beginnings and endings. Rather, he was always on the move, and visited Jerusalem when he needed to, not for a rest from being a missionary. The whole 'missionary journey' notion is a modern deduction from Acts, but Acts leaves large gaps in its account, as we know from a comparison with the letters. It also streamlines the story, aiming to give not a full history of the early church nor even of Paul's part in it, but to show how the Christian message spread triumphantly, despite all obstacles, from its cradle in Jerusalem to its new centre as a world faith in Rome.

One important difference between Acts and Paul concerns his status as an apostle. Although more than half of Acts is about Paul as a great hero, it does not call him an apostle except in 14: 4, 14 (where, however, he is bracketed with Barnabas). For Acts, apostles are normally the Twelve, of whom Paul is not one (see 1: 15–26), and he cannot be called an apostle in the same sense. Yet Paul does claim for himself apostleship in the same sense as for Peter, though aware that not everyone concedes the point (see 1 Cor. 9: 1f.; 15: 1–11; Gal. 1: 1, 17 and cf. 1 Thess. 2: 6; Rom. 1: 1, 5). The exact meaning of 'apostle' in early Christianity is much debated, but clearly Paul regards himself as no whit inferior to any other apostle in status and authority. If having been a witness of the risen Christ is the necessary condition for being an apostle, then he qualifies, for his experience on the Damascus road was a resurrection appearance of the same kind and in the same series as those to Peter and the others (1 Cor. 9: 1; 15: 1–11). Nevertheless, the essential qualification in his view is the divine call and commission (Gal. 1 and 2) to apostleship which gave him his authority.

Letters

Paul wrote neither theological treatises nor sermons but letters. In Greek culture — as often in ours — the letter was a substitute for personal presence, and Paul's letters are substitutes for authoritative apostolic presence. They were meant to be received as he would have been, just as sometimes an emissary is to be regarded as a substitute for his presence (see 1 Cor. 4: 14–21; 2 Cor. 12: 14–13: 13; 1 Thess. 2: 17–3: 5). They are real letters, and so are directed to specific people in specific situations. Obvious though this may be, it needs saying because of its consequences.

First, Paul writes pastorally rather than systematically. For example, he nowhere gives a thorough account of the relation between the Law and the gospel, but deals with problems involving them as they arise. To the Galatians, he concentrates on Christians' freedom from the Law, but to the Corinthians, he is preoccupied with the need for righteous living. This difference reflects the different situations and problems of the two churches at the times of writing. Paul consistently goes to first principles, and is an acute and creative theological thinker, but he is before that a missionary pastor giving his attention to concrete problems. All his theology comes to us in this way.

Secondly, we cannot too readily compare something in one letter with something in another, without taking account of the differing circumstances. We cannot just collect everything he says on a topic without regard for the contexts. Yet we must also be prepared for an underlying coherence and consistency in what he writes.

Thirdly, we are in the position of hearing only one side of a conversation, and can only deduce from what Paul says *to* a church what he must have heard *from* them. For example, in 1 Cor. 7: 1, 'It is well for a man not to touch a woman', is that what he is saying to the Corinthians, or is he quoting what they had said to him? In fact it is probably the latter. Moreover, why are the Corinthians proud of their wisdom, lax about incest, yet inclined towards asceticism, divided about eating food offered to idols, unsure about the resurrection, and so on? Is there a coherent position behind this strange assortment of ideas? Similar questions can be asked of all the letters, and answers often boil down to two. Sometimes Paul faces the problem of people who think Christians ought all to keep the Jewish Law, as in Galatians, Romans, and Philippians. Sometimes he faces those inclined to a kind of religion which later crystallized into something called Gnosticism (see pp. 15–17), as conceivably in the Corinthian letters. Certainly there will be times when interpretation is affected by the target we suppose Paul to be aiming at.

Fourthly, Paul writes to Christians, and his letters are not in themselves missionary preaching. Yet there are occasional allusions to what he preached, as in 1 Cor. 15: 3ff.: the death and resurrection of Jesus Christ, in fulfilment of the Scriptures, and his appearances (see also Gal. 3: 1). Generally, however, the letters take the preaching for granted and go on from there.

Now when we say that Paul wrote real letters, we do not mean modern ones. Much work has recently been done, especially in the

United States, on the structure of Paul's letters in comparison with roughly contemporary letters. It has been shown that whatever their purpose and subject matter, letters had substantially the same structure. The Pauline form is:

Salutation (names of writer and recipient; greeting)
Thanksgiving
Opening of the body of the letter
Body of the letter (usually in two parts, theoretical and practical)
Closing of the body of the letter (often with the promise of a
  visit)
Ethical instruction ('paraenesis')
Closing: greetings, doxology, benediction.

Obviously the proportions may vary, and an element may on occasion be mising, but if so there is a reason. An outstanding case of a missing element is in Galatians, where there is no opening thanksgiving, despite the fact that Paul's Christian thanksgivings reflect the common good manners of secular letters. Paul is so furious with his Galatian readers for their lack of fidelity to the gospel as they had received it that he has no time or inclination for thanksgiving, whatever politeness dictated.

Moreover, this pattern can be used to help detect whether a letter now exists in the form in which Paul wrote it. Some letters may be composite, put together by an editor from fragments. Neither 2 Corinthians nor Philippians fits the pattern quite satisfactorily, and this is a strong, though not by itself conclusive, reason to regard them as composite. Certainly there is widespread agreement that the letters are not constructed haphazardly as used to be thought, but conform to the contemporary letter-pattern.

The recipients of the letters were of course Christians, but were they mainly Jewish Christians or Gentile Christians or Gentiles who had already been adherents of a Jewish synagogue without becoming converts? Undoubtedly many were Gentiles (non-Jews), which in practice meant they were Greek in culture and language. In nearly every letter this emerges somewhere (e.g. Rom. 11: 13; 1 Cor. 8: 7; Gal. 4: 8; Phil. 3: 3; 1 Thess. 1: 9). Moreover, although the gospel came 'first to the Jew and then to the Greek' (e.g. Rom. 1: 16), and despite the pattern in Acts where he begins in the synagogue and moves out only under pressure, Paul sees his mission as specifically to the Gentiles. He is 'an apostle to the Gentiles' (Rom. 11: 13; 15: 16; Gal. 1: 16) by divine appointment. Thus it is likely that his churches were composed largely of Gentiles, but some may well have had a period as synagogue-adherents, and there were probably Jews too, because Paul can take for granted a knowledge of the Septuagint. He assumes his readers will know about Adam and Abraham, Moses and circumcision, and will recognize scriptural quotations and allusions. Because of the great cost, it is unlikely that individuals or young churches would have possessed copies, and it is only in the synagogue that this familiarity with the Scriptures in Greek could have been gained.

Sources for the knowledge of Paul's thought

We have seen that some letters may have been compiled by a later hand; others, at least as we now have them, may have been *composed* by a later follower or group of followers of Paul. This question will concern us in Chapter 7, though for a full treatment one should go to standard books like W. G. Kümmel's *Introduction to the New Testament*. Meanwhile, we need to know which letters we can use confidently as sources, which with no confidence at all, and which come somewhere in between, and we also need to know about the Acts of the Apostles.

First, we use Acts only as a subsidiary source. This is because it is proper to prefer a primary source (i.e. coming from the person himself) to a secondary source (i.e. evidence about that person from someone else). A second reason for caution is that both in chronology and in the account given of Paul's teaching, Acts is difficult to reconcile with the letters and appears to give an inadequate or even distorted picture of both. At the very least it leaves large gaps, both in time and in theology, for some of which see Chapter 7.

Secondly, of the letters ascribed to Paul we can confidently use Romans, 1 and 2 Corinthians, Galatians, Philippians, 1 Thessalonians and Philemon. Some may not be in their original form, but few doubt that Paul wrote them. On the remaining letters, again see Chapter 7. We shall not be using them a great deal because, even if they are written by Paul, it is an older Paul whose thought and style have changed. Hebrews, of course, does not even claim to be by him.

The order in which they were written is of some importance, especially if we suspect that Paul's thought developed over the years. Unfortunately there is great uncertainty about the order, as there is about the chronology of the apostle's life. At the risk of being arbitrary, however, we need to give some indication of probable order and in rough outline some notion of time scale. It is generally agreed that there are three groups of letters:

1. Early letters: 1 and 2 Thessalonians (unless the latter is not by Paul).

2. The great letters: Romans, 1 and 2 Corinthians, Galatians, and perhaps Philippians.

3. 'Captivity' letters: Philemon, Colossians, Ephesians, and perhaps Philippians.

If Paul wrote them all, then Group 1 were written about 50, Group 2 in the middle to late 50s, and Group 3 in the early 60s, but almost every date is disputed and some would argue that all the letters in Group 3 are either not by Paul or not written from Rome. Again, many put Galatians in Group 1 rather than 2, and some put all the dates a good deal earlier. Nevertheless, as long as we do not pretend to precision, we have a reasonable idea of the time-span, namely the 50s and early 60s of the first century.

2

Paul's Inheritance

If we are to understand Paul, we must take note of the culture and the religious traditions in which he stood. He had conceptual and linguistic equipment that his hearers took for granted, but which is strange to us. Moreover, he lived within a mixing of cultures, arising from the Macedonian conquests under Alexander the Great in the Fourth Century BC. Thereafter, the Mediterranean world was always partly Greek, whatever else it was. Yet the conquered had their revenge on the conquerors, and Greek religion, culture, and thought were infiltrated by oriental ideas and practices. This whole phenomenon is what we call Hellenism: the Greek culture of the Graeco-Roman world as a whole, not that of Greece of the classical age.

An apparent exception to this mutual influence was Israel, which ostensibly resisted all attempts at cultural imperialism and religious syncretism in order to keep the nation pure and uncontaminated under God. It is evident, however, that while pious Jews were holding the front door shut against foreign pressure, the back window was open enough to let mixing take place. This means that the distinction we shall make between Jewish and Hellenistic influences on Paul must not be taken too rigidly. Even Palestinian Judaism was penetrated by alien elements, often unconsciously. Moreover, what follows is far from pretending to be a thorough description of the competing forces.

Paul's Jewish inheritance and eschatological framework

Paul not only had been a Jew; he remained one. His 'conversion' was not from Judaism, but from what he came to regard as an outmoded form of it, to what he believed was its true fulfilment.

So, while he rejected some aspects of his past (Phil. 3: 4–11), he never ceased seeing himself as part of Israel (Rom. 9–11, especially 11:1), and he simply takes for granted a Jewish framework without feeling any need to spell it out.

Paul assumes without argument the Jewish belief in only one God, even though he refers to it explicitly only rarely (e.g. Gal. 3: 20). He speaks of polytheism with the same horror and sense of absurdity that we meet, for example, in Isa. 44 (see Rom. 1: 22–32). God may have agents and messengers such as angels (Gal. 1: 8), and his activity may be spoken of in personal terms using Wisdom language (see Chapter 3 below), but these never threaten the oneness and monarchy of God. In this Paul stands with his fathers. Moreover, this God's operations are to be discerned in history. God called Abraham, sent him to find a new land, and promised he would be a means of blessing to the whole world through a son (Rom. 4; Gal. 3). God made a covenant with Israel, gave her the Law to enable her to live within that covenant, having first rescued her from Egypt (Rom. 9: 4), and later spoke through the prophets (Rom. 1: 17). No more than most of his contemporaries does he speculate about this God, but like them he discovers him in his saving activity.

Like many other Jews, he believed history was divided into aeons (ages), especially the present evil age in which God's rightful authority is flouted and sin is rampant, and a new age when the divine sovereignty will be reasserted and universally acknowledged, all wrongs will be righted and all the oppressed liberated. A simple form of this view of history had long existed, originally looking for national restoration in political, moral, and religious terms. We find this hope from the time of the exile, when a shattered and displaced people longed for return from captivity, but for a return with a difference, not just a resumption of the old uncertain loyalties and divided devotion. Rather, they looked for a renewal of life in all its aspects, of a kind which only God could accomplish. (See Jer. 30–33 and Isa. 40–55). This hope (usually called 'eschatological' meaning 'to do with the End') was later in some circles replaced by a more complicated and more radical one. This later form of hope (usually called 'apocalyptic' which means 'uncovering', because it revealed God's hitherto secret purposes) could take various shapes. Usually, however, it looked for a new aeon that was not a renewal of the present aeon, but its radical replacement. It looked for a new heaven and a new earth, a divine kingdom on a cosmic rather than a national scale, in which the old world would be swept away and righteousness, peace, and truth remain.

One regular element was the hope of resurrection. Those who believed in life after death at all, tended in the Palestinian tradition to believe in a general resurrection at the End, a resurrection to Judgment, when God would make his decisions on human beings. Thus anyone reared in this tradition who heard of the resurrection of Jesus would be apt to conclude that the general resurrection had begun and that the End was on the doorstep. The gift of the Spirit of God was another mark of the age: God would breathe not just on a few special servants, but on all his people. To talk as Christians did about the presence of the Holy Spirit implied at least the beginning of the new age. Again, although the Messiah belonged more naturally to the simpler nationalistic hope than to the cosmic apocalyptic one, he too could represent the End time. All together, these central elements in the Christian message must be understood in this eschatological or apocalyptic setting. See also Chapter 5.

Paul assumes also the traditionally positive Jewish attitude to the world as God's creation and therefore good. The saving God is also the Creator and this world is still his despite contamination by sin and rebellious forces. God is to be found within it, its pleasures, pains, and its physical nature, not by fleeing it. The misuse of the created world and of human appetites is sinful, but their proper use and enjoyment are neither sinful nor inferior. When dealing with scrupulosity about what Christians can and cannot eat, Paul quotes with approval Ps. 24: 1, 'The earth is the Lord's, and everything in it.' See 1 Cor. 10: 26.

This leads us to Paul's 'anthropology' (his understanding of the nature of human beings). Paul inherited an Old Testament view of human beings as wholes, though having different aspects, and not as consisting of two quite different parts, physical and non-physical, body and soul. The emphasis was on the totality, not on parts, and many Jews found it impossible to conceive of existence without embodiment. This is why the hope for life after death was characteristically resurrection and not the immortality of the soul (though in some circles affected by Greek thinking the latter was found, for example in Wisd. 3: 1ff). A disembodied existence was equivalent to nakedness (2 Cor. 5: 3f). As a result when we meet terms like 'flesh' and 'spirit' we cannot assume that Paul means the physical and bad as against the inward and good (e.g. Gal. 5: 17). In fact he means two different orientations of the whole person, towards or away from God, as we shall see in Chapter 5. For Paul and for the Jewish tradition, the created world and the physical person are the scene of God's redemption, not the prison from which humanity is to be rescued.

Paul assumes that God's activity in history is channelled through the agency of a particular people. God does care for all nations, but this care is expressed through Israel (cf. Isa. 42: 6; 49: 6). As this channel and servant, Israel had a special place, but not because of her merits, rather because of God's gracious decision (cf. Deut. 7: 6–8). Jesus the Messiah came into this chosen people as its fulfilment: 'to them belong the sonship, the glory, the covenants, the giving of the law, the worship, and the promises; to them belong the patriarchs, and of their race, according to the flesh, is the Christ.' (Rom. 9: 4f). His own people's rejection of him as Messiah raised agonizing problems for Paul as a Jewish Christian (see Rom. 9–11).

Inseparable from covenant and election was the Torah (the law and the traditions, initially as contained in the Pentateuch). This was a major problem for Paul, because if as he believed Gentiles were now called into the people of God, were they also called to obey the Law of that covenant people? He was sure they were not, but then what becomes of the Law as the divinely provided guidance for God's people? The question was the more acute because Paul had been a Pharisee, one of the largely lay group who took obedience to the Law with the utmost seriousness and who strove to keep it relevant to new situations and new questions by a process of explanation and interpretation. In Paul's time this was entirely oral, but it was eventually written down in the Mishnah and related works. A static and remote Law would not do. If one is to 'remember the Sabbath day to keep it holy' one needs guidance. How do we keep it holy? By doing no work. What constitutes work: cooking, washing, walking? The questions are endless but important, especially where there is a determination to maintain detailed observance within the spirit of the original command. The oral tradition of the Pharisees was designed not to make life burdensome, but to help the ordinary person to know how to live within the divine will. Its intention was populist, not elitist, and is what Paul is talking about in Gal. 1: 13f when he says how zealous he was for 'the traditions of my fathers'.

In Paul's time Pharisaism was one option alongside Sadducaism, or Essenism, or simply avoiding such religious seriousness. But this is the sort of Jew Paul was, 'circumcised on the eighth day, of the people of Israel, of the tribe of Benjamin, a Hebrew born of Hebrews; as to the law a Pharisee, as to zeal a persecutor of the church, as to righteousness under the law blameless' (Phil. 3: 5–6). His persecuting of Christians thus arose from his concern for the Law. Jews who were lax about it endangered the nation, whose health and success were believed to depend on its keeping the Law.

Paul's Jewishness emerges in more detailed ways also. Like most Rabbis, he had a trade and supported himself by it on occasions though not always (compare 1 Thess. 2: 9 with 2 Cor. 11: 7–9 and Phil. 4: 15, 18). He never says what his work was, but Acts 18: 3 says he made tents. More important is that he handles Old Testament passages like a Rabbi, treating them as authoritative, but also stringing them together (e.g. Rom. 3: 10–18, and often in Rom. 9–11). All his ways of introducing quotations are paralleled in early Jewish writings: for example 'for it is written' (Gal. 3: 13) or 'the scripture says' (Rom. 4: 3).

Paul's debt to his Pharisaic Jewish heritage scarcely needs further stress. His own words, and his evident dependence on it for his theological agenda, speak for themselves.

The Hellenistic inheritance

We can mention only a few aspects of this complex phenomenon which by the Roman period impinged not just on the aristocracy but on the ordinary people of Palestine. Religiously, it tended towards polytheism and the use of images, though there were strongly monotheistic strands too. The polytheistic religion was closely connected with cultural institutions like the Games and the Gymnasium, so that participation in them tended to imply endorsement of the religion. Philosophically, though sharp distinctions between Greek and Hebrew ways of thought can no longer be made, there was a greater skill in the use of abstraction than in traditional Jewish culture. Roughly speaking, the Jew thought of God in terms of what he did, and the Greek in terms of his nature, what he was. Moreover, there was a Hellenistic tradition which saw divinity and humanity as not fundamentally too dissimilar, one being a lofty or even promoted form of the other. So there could be demi-gods, and divine men, and a great figure like an emperor could be deified after his death or even before it.

How much was Paul affected by Hellenism? First, he writes fluently and naturally in Greek. His language often reflects the Septuagint in quotation, allusion, and in the meanings given to words, but on the whole it fits well into the common Greek of the time. It is often said that as a native of Tarsus, a notable Hellenistic centre, and as a Roman citizen, he must have grown up well-versed in contemporary pagan culture, see Acts 9: 11; 21: 39; 22: 3; also 16: 37f; 22: 25–9; 23: 27. Yet if these factors were so important, it is odd that Paul never mentions them, and in any case being born and brought up in a cultural metropolis does not necessarily mean sharing in its riches. Pious Jews were as capable then as now of insulating themselves from what they saw as godlessness, but there is a real possibility that Paul's upbringing was in Jerusalem not Tarsus; Acts 22: 3 can be read that way, and whenever he talks about his background he gives the impression that it was thoroughly Jewish and Palestinian (see for example Phil. 3: 4–6). We therefore cannot be sure that he grew up as a man of two worlds, Jewish and Hellenistic, but we know that he became such a man, who moved about the Hellenistic world a great deal and whose letters show him aware of its culture. Some indications are trivial: he appears in 1 Cor. 15: 33 to quote the poet Menander, though the saying may have become proverbial; 2 Cor. 4: 18 may reflect the Platonic view that unseen things are more real than seen things; 'conscience', rarely to be found in even contemporary Jewish writings, may well have entered his vocabulary — he uses it about fourteen times — from Stoic philosophy at least in a popularized form; 'content' (in Greek *autarkēs*, 'self-sufficient') in Phil. 4: 11 may also derive from Stoicism, though for Paul sufficiency is not in ourselves but in God. In no instance can we be sure he is aware of his indebtedness, and in none is there any sign of formative influence on him. We now turn to some areas where such formative influence has been supposed.

Mystery religions

Although these reached the peak of their popularity in the Roman world in all probability somewhat later, they were already thriving in Paul's day. They varied considerably, but had some common features, though we have to be cautious in trying to delineate those features because we are dealing with essentially secret matters. In a society where official religion could tend to be formal, and be primarily aimed at maintaining the well-being of that society, the mysteries served to provide their initiates with a rich religious experience. It has often been said that they offered identification with a god through death and rebirth with that deity, and that they promised an enhancement of life not only in the present but also after death. Certainly the notion of life through death was common in the ancient world in initiations and in rites of passage, and by no means only in the mystery religions. Yet it now appears that the idea of death and subsequent rebirth (let alone resurrection) *with the god* is not to be found in these cults, at least not in the First Century. Indeed the mystery religions seem not to have used the language of resurrection for initiates at all, let alone in identification with a god. What they did promise was life under the power of the god, life here and hereafter. There were many such cults, and we know all too little about them. Among the best-known were those of Cybele, Eleusis, Isis, and Mithras. Most probably originated in the east as fertility cults to ensure the crops for the coming year, but such origins had long since been forgotten.

When Paul in 1 Cor. 8: 5f talks about 'many gods and many lords' he may be thinking of these cults, and the Christian sacraments of baptism and the eucharist may possibly indicate their impact. Above all it has been argued that in speaking of dying and rising with Christ, as in Rom. 6, he is presenting Christianity as such a cult. Yet the parallels are not as close as they at first seem. Unlike the cults, Paul mostly speaks of resurrection rather than rebirth. Unlike them, he invites participation in a real event of the recent past, not in a timeless but ever true death and rebirth. Above all, the basic orientation is different. In baptism, the fundamental thing is entry into the New Age inaugurated by the death and resurrection of Jesus the Messiah, meaning that those who belong to him are already tasting in advance the powers and reality of that New Age. Similarly, while the eucharist could be seen as a ritual sharing in the cult deity, it is more plausibly to be interpreted as a foretaste of the messianic banquet, the feast of the New Age, which is enjoyed by those who renounce the old age ('dying') and embrace the new by anticipation ('rising'). Rom. 6 on baptism and 1 Cor. 11 on the eucharist both fit more naturally into an eschatological and Jewish framework than into one derived from the Hellenistic mysteries. Nevertheless similarities do exist, and it is hard to believe that they never occurred to Paul or his readers.

Gnosticism

This was not simply a particular set of beliefs, but a movement, a way of looking at God, self, and the world, which took many forms, whose roots were at least partly in Judaism. Perhaps the crucial thing was its view of a higher self as basically and permanently alien to the physical world and the physical person. Gnostics ('knowers') felt themselves to be in a prison from which they must and could escape. They believed that many human beings consist of a fragment or spark of the divine which has somehow been displaced and imprisoned in a totally alien physical world and body. Others are merely rational but animal, having no spark of divinity in them. The fragments have a longing for reunion not only with each other, but also with the high divinity or primal divine Anthropos (Man) from which they were broken off in some pre-cosmic fall. The high God is certainly not the creator, for creation was either an appalling blunder carried out in ignorance by an inferior deity, or the work of a malevolent power. Neither the high God nor the enlightened person (Gnostic) has any business with the creator or his work.

Various stories ('myths') were told in order to explain how this tragic state of affairs came about. Further, some have thought that in Paul's day there already existed stories of a heavenly redeemer, sent from the realm of pure spirit in which the fragments originated, at great danger to himself, in order to tell them of their true nature and to prepare them for the ascent to their true home after death. Sometimes this redeemer is thought of as the original Anthropos from which the fragments were separated, but in any case his function is to reveal the knowledge (*Gnōsis*) of their real nature to his hearers and to reassemble himself, restoring his primordial perfection. The fragments can thus rise to the world of light and spirit as components of the divine fullness and unity.

Now it has been suggested that this story underlies Paul's description of Christ as redeemer, especially in Phil. 2: 6–11 (cf. Col. 1: 15–20). More commonly it is thought that such views were held by his opponents, especially in Corinth, but that Paul rejected them because for him Creator and Redeemer were linked as Father and Son, and because he could not regard the physical body and the physical world as intrinsically hostile to God and true humanity. Further, he never envisaged believers' losing their identity in the Redeemer. There is, however, little evidence for this Redeemer Myth as a whole before the third century AD, and it is unlikely that Gnosticism became an elaborated system until a century after Paul. We ought not, therefore, to read back a later system into his letters without more evidence.

There is great difficulty in pinpointing Hellenism's influence on Paul, even though nobody doubts its existence. To take another case, he sometimes refers to malevolent powers which rank somewhere between Satan and the demons. There was a pervading contemporary belief in such powers and in their influence on the world's affairs. Nations and social groupings had their own 'guardian angels' to protect them, to control their destinies, and to work against their enemies. At least where Christians are concerned, these powers are now ineffective, for Christ triumphed over them on the cross (see Rom. 8: 38f; 1 Cor. 2: 6, 8; Gal. 4: 3, 8f; perhaps Rom. 13: 1; cf. Col. 2: 20). Did this idea come from Paul's Hellenistic environment? It seems unlikely, for Judaism had a similar idea even in the Old Testament (see Deut. 32: 8; Dan. 10: 13, 20f; 12: 1), and is the more ready source of Paul's conception.

He does, of course, use literary devices familiar to his Hellenistic readers. For example, on several occasions he conducts a running debate with an imaginary opponent whose arguments and objections are promptly countered (see especially Rom. 2 and 3). Though some doubts have arisen, it is likely that he is employing the Hellenistic device known as the diatribe. Certainly his freedom and skill in writing included rhetoric.

Hellenistic Judaism

A major reason why it is so difficult to identify precise examples of the impact of Hellenism on Paul is that Judaism itself had already felt the same impact, even in Palestine. Consequently it is frequently impossible to determine whether a given piece of his theological equipment has come from one source rather than the other. It may be too much to say that all Judaism was Hellenistic, yet a sharp division between traditionalist Judaism in Palestine and Hellenistic Judaism in the Dispersion will no longer serve. Probably much Judaism outside Palestine was as conservative as much inside, and within Palestine little if any was entirely free from Hellenistic influence. Even the words 'synagogue' and 'Sanhedrin' are Greek, and the Qumran sect which fiercely resisted the infiltration of foreign ideas and was rigidly devoted to Yahweh, yet betrays signs of the impact of Hellenism.

Nevertheless there was a strand of Judaism, particularly associated with Alexandria and with Philo, in which the process is seen most sharply and most explicitly. Here, Jewish thinking appears in a markedly Hellenistic dress (or vice versa). In his very large literary output, Philo sometimes seems the conventional Jew, but sometimes a philosopher of a fundamentally Platonic character. In re-telling Old Testament stories, he makes them allegories of philosophical ideas. To take an example, when Abraham leaves his homeland for the new land God had promised him, this is a representation of the soul's leaving the body and the world of the senses for the world of true spiritual reality (*de Migr. Abr.* 1ff). Philo was not an isolated figure, though he is the chief and by far the most prolific exponent of a tendency to marry Israel's religious tradition with the philosophy of the Greeks. The purpose was partly to defend Judaism in terms that Hellenists could understand, against charges of irrationality and barbarism, and so to commend it to thinking pagans inclined towards monotheism, but perhaps partly also to provide Jews with a way out of an intellectual ghetto.

Such Jews read the Torah in Greek translation, and so apparently did Paul. It can be shown that in his quotations he usually employs the Septuagint, or something very close to it, rather than the Hebrew. This does not in itself make him a Hellenistic Jew, but merely shows that he moved in circles where it was the Greek Old Testament that was known. His quoting must have been mostly from memory, for he could scarcely carry a bulky and expensive copy around with him. It is therefore particularly interesting that what he remembers is the Septuagint. Again, in his use of words and in the meanings he gives them, he is under its influence. What we need to know, however, is whether there is any evidence that his thinking was influenced by people like Philo, or the Hellenistic Jewish 'Wisdom of Solomon'. It is hard to be sure. His attack on idolatry in Rom. 1: 18–32 is rather like that in Wisd. 12–14, but there are differences, and direct dependence is uncertain. In his allegorical piece about Hagar, Sarah, and their sons in Gal. 4: 21–31, he writes somewhat like Philo, but Hellenistic Judaism had no monopoly of allegory; it can be found in the Old Testament (Ezek. 15–17) and in later Palestinian Judaism. Even his use of the figure of Wisdom to convey teaching about Christ (see pp. 32–5), does not of itself show dependence on the Judaism of the Dispersion and the Hellenistic world rather than of Palestine.

It is worth repeating that when Paul does talk about the sort of Judaism in which he lived, as in Phil. 3: 5f; Gal. 1: 14f, it all sounds thoroughly Palestinian and traditional.

The Christian inheritance

Though a Jew working in a Hellenistic environment and often using Hellenistic tools, Paul belonged to a Christian tradition, however young it must have been when he was called. In Gal. 1: 11f he seems to say that his knowledge of the Christian message came entirely by divine revelation, and that he received no Christian instruction or tradition from others. This is incredible. He himself a few verses later mentions spending a fortnight with Cephas (Peter) in Jerusalem, and it is impossible to believe that they *never* mentioned the tradition about Jesus or the Jerusalem church's preaching. More probably he is referring in Gal. 1: 11f to his particular understanding of the Christian message, especially his attitude to the Law as not needing to be kept by Gentile converts. Certainly he inherited the practices of baptism and the eucharist, and takes them for granted as established in his churches (1 Cor. 1: 13–17; Rom. 6: 3; and 1 Cor. 10: 16–21; 11: 23–6).

On occasion he specifically quotes or refers to early Christian tradition. In discussing the eucharist in 1 Cor. 11: 23–6 he begins: 'For I received from the Lord what I also delivered to you, that the Lord Jesus on the night when he was betrayed took bread . . .' The words 'received' and 'delivered' are those used for the handing on of a tradition, and so Paul means that he received this tradition in the normal human way, but that its ultimate origin is the Lord Jesus Christ. He can scarcely mean that he had a special divine revelation about it; all he needed to do was ask a question. Again, we have already noted that he quotes Christian tradition in 1 Cor. 15: 3ff, and other passages of differing degrees of probability can be added, including Rom. 1: 3f; 3: 21–6; and the triad faith, hope, and love: compare 1 Cor. 13: 13 and 1 Thess. 1: 3 with 1 Pet. 1: 21f and Heb. 10: 22–4. The 'Christ-hymn' in Phil. 2: 6–11 may well be a quotation annotated by Paul, and there was also even before him an ethical as well as a preaching tradition as he hints in 1 Thess. 4: 1f; 1 Cor. 11: 2; Rom. 6: 17. Moreover, in the New Testament as in contemporary Stoic and Hellenistic Jewish writing, ethical teaching tends to occur in stock forms, lists of virtues and vices, and codes telling how to behave within one's social position: wives and husbands, parents and children, slaves and masters (and, within the church, leaders and led). These conventional forms are more evident in later Christian writings, but we do find lists in Gal. 5: 19–23, and the beginning of codes in Rom. 13: 1–7 and 1 Cor. 7: 17–24 (see also Col. 3: 18 — 4:1).

How far was he indebted to the tradition of the deeds and words of Jesus? Form criticism assumes that the early church continually used the Jesus-material, adapting it and even creating it to meet the concrete needs of debate, witness, preaching, and instruction. We should expect to perceive distinct echoes of this in Paul, yet he betrays astonishingly little knowledge of or even interest in the traditions about Jesus. This is one of the strangest and most puzzling areas of early Christian history. Of course he frequently speaks of the cross and resurrection, but of the life of Jesus he tells us only:

that Jesus was a Jew born of a woman under the Jewish Law (Gal. 3: 16; 4: 4);

that he was of the line of David (Rom. 1: 3);

that his ministry was essentially to Israel (Rom. 15: 8);

that he had a meal with his disciples, including a betrayer, on the eve of his death, commanding them to continue such meals in remembrance of him (1 Cor. 11: 23–5).

There appears equally little of the teaching of Jesus. In 1 Cor. 7: 10 (unlike vv. 12, 25 where he says he has no dominical command) it is not he but the Lord who commands that husbands and wives stay with their spouses. This is usually taken to refer to the teaching about divorce found variously in Matt. 19: 6, Mark 10: 9, and Luke 16: 18. Yet he does not feel bound to follow it to the letter, and allows exceptions (1 Cor. 7: 11). In 1 Cor. 9: 14 'the Lord commanded that those who proclaim the gospel should get their living by the gospel' is thought to reflect the tradition of Matt. 10: 10 and Luke 10: 7, 'the labourer deserves his wages'. Yet here too Paul does not feel bound to put it into practice (v. 12). Apart from a possible but very vague connection between 1 Thess. 4: 15f and Mark 13: 26f, there are no other direct references to the words of Jesus in the letters of Paul.

There may, however, be unattributed quotations, and certainly there are some clear parallels to gospel material in some passages of ethical instruction. One famous example is Rom. 12–13 where many echoes have been detected, such as 'Bless those who persecute you . . .' (Rom. 12: 14; cf. Matt. 5: 44 and Luke 6: 28) and 'Repay no one evil for evil . . .' (Rom. 12: 17; cf. Matt. 5: 39) and '. . . love is the fulfilling of the law' (Rom. 13: 8–10; cf. Matt. 22: 34–40 and parallels). The wording is never identical, there is no acknowledgement of source, and no distinction between 'gospel' material and the rest. These things are true also of another rich source of parallels with gospel material, 1 Thess. 4–5, including 'Be at peace among yourselves' (1 Thess. 5: 13; cf. Mark 9: 50) and 'See that none of you repays evil for evil' (1 Thess. 5: 15; cf. Matt. 5: 39 and Rom. 12: 17). The similarities and parallels cannot be disputed. Further, no one doubts the closeness of Paul's attitudes to those of Jesus in the gospels: we may think of his use of 'Abba' in prayer (compare Rom. 8: 15 and Gal. 4: 6 with Mark 14: 36) or we may compare what Paul says about circumcision in Galatians with the rejection of food laws in Mark 7: 14–23.

The really odd thing is that in the overwhelming majority of cases Paul either does not know he is echoing the Jesus tradition, or, if he knows, chooses not to acknowledge his indebtedness.

If in Rom. 12 he is heavily influenced by the material we know from Matt. 5, as many think, why does he not increase the impact and authority of his appeal by saying so? We have seen that on a very few occasions (1 Cor. 7: 10; 9: 14) he can invoke the authority of the Lord, but why not more often? This is one of the great conundrums in the study of Paul.

Does he refer so little to Jesus' words and deeds because he has covered it in his preaching? There is little to say so, even in Acts: Acts 13: 16–41 comes closest, but even here there is not much. Anyway this would not explain why he can almost quote, without acknowledgement. Does 2 Cor. 5: 16 ('. . . even though we once regarded Christ from a human point of view, we regard him thus no longer') show that he deliberately rejects all preoccupation with the historical Jesus and is concerned only with the exalted Lord? This verse, on the contrary, concerns the kind of knowledge, not its object. It is the viewpoint which is no longer merely human, or 'fleshly' as the Greek has it. Some point out that Paul does show an acquaintance with the character of Jesus, his humility and obedience to God, as in Phil. 2: 6–11; 2 Cor. 8: 9; 10: 1; Rom. 15: 3, 8. However, the reference is usually to his enduring the cross, rather than to his life as such.

In the end we are reduced to two alternative explanations. First, that Paul did not know the Jesus-tradition in any detail. He did not attribute quotations and allusions because he did not know which pieces of teaching were supposed to originate with Jesus and which were not. If this explanation is correct, then in view of his having spent a fortnight with Peter (Gal. 1: 18) it must follow that the primitive church was *not* intensely preoccupied with the use and transmission of the Jesus-tradition. If, despite his opportunities to learn it, Paul knew little of it, it can hardly have had a central place in the life of the Jerusalem church.

The alternative explanation is that Paul had little interest in the Jesus-tradition. He concentrated on Jesus crucified, risen, and exalted, the present reigning and saving Lord now active through the Spirit. This, and not stories about Jesus and his teaching, was what mattered. In teaching, he relied more on the present direction of the Spirit in the church than on words of Jesus from the past.

The church's authority was not the teacher of Galilee but the risen Lord speaking through the Spirit. He does not attribute quotations because it is not important to do so. What matters is what God is saying now. In many ways this is theologically attractive, but few have been entirely happy with it, if only because on a very few occasions he can quote Jesus-sayings without qualms.

The problem is unsolved, but it shows that there was in any case a greater variety of attitudes to the Jesus-tradition than we should have expected. The Gospel of Matthew's emphasis on Jesus as a great Rabbi or teacher is virtually absent from Paul. Christ's redemptive death, resurrection, and present lordship, fill Paul's horizon. Whether by design or accident, the teaching and deeds of Jesus of Nazareth are virtually ignored.

Paul remained a Jew, at home in the Hellenistic world. He became a Christian, entering into an already existing tradition. The crucial moment in the making of the Paul whose letters we read, however, was an experience which he believed was an encounter with Christ himself.

3

The Centrality of Jesus Christ

Paul did not become a Christian because he had come to the end of his tether as a Jew. He was a happy and zealous Jew whose new belief that Jesus was the answer to human dilemmas made him find inadequacies in the Judaism that had hitherto satisfied him. The main reason for doubting this is a particular reading of Rom. 7, especially vv. 13–24, which takes it as autobiographical and as describing the moral impotence he experienced when he tried to keep the Law. On this reading, Paul knew from the Law what he ought to do, tried to do it, and failed. Only when Christ came to him did he find escape from this impotence and enter new life (v. 25). Throughout the passage, from v. 7, the occurrence of 'I' makes it natural to take it all autobiographically, so why not?

It is quite uncertain whether Rom. 7: 13–24 describes divided life as a Christian, as a Jew, or as Jew from a Christian vantage point, but we may concede that the last rather than the first is the most likely. The logic of the letter suggests that in Chap. 7 he is talking about one of the things from which people are delivered by Christ, and it is difficult to suppose that he thinks Christians are as impotent and imprisoned by sinfulness as the chapter depicts. Granted this, however, it does not follow that he is talking about himself in particular or about how life under the Law seemed at the time. He is talking about options —bondage or freedom — as they seem now, not as they seemed then. The use of 'I' is rhetorical for human beings generally, and does not focus on one human being in particular. Moreover, other evidence shows that when he was a traditional Jew he experienced no such dilemma. This is seen above all in avowedly autobiographical passages: 'I advanced in Judaism beyond many of my own age, so extremely zealous was I for the traditions of my fathers'

(Gal. 1: 14); and 'as to the law a Pharisee, as to zeal a persecutor of the church, as to righteousness under the law blameless.' (Phil. 3: 5f). Thus while we cannot entirely rule out all reflection of his own experience from Rom. 7, the passage is not primarily autobiographical (for further discussion see below, Chapter 6).

When he looks back as a Christian he finds this zeal and righteousness to be not good enough, but the end of Phil. 3: 6 seems to establish that at the time he was content as a Jew, not unduly burdened by feelings of guilt. In fact he seems not to have proceeded from a deeply felt problem to a solution in Christ, but the other way round: he first accepted Christ as centre and solution, and then saw with new eyes what the problem was. It was only when he had been liberated that he understood his bondage.

The call

Paul first met Christianity as its opponent. Acts and his letters put this beyond question. He wanted to eradicate 'the church of God' (Gal. 1: 13) from the Jewish community because he believed Christians were bad Jews, betraying their heritage and their God. In Phil. 3: 5f 'as to zeal a persecutor of the church' is sandwiched between 'as to the law a Pharisee' and 'as to righteousness under the law blameless'. Moreover Jesus could not be the Messiah, for a hanged man is under a curse from God (Deut. 21: 23; Gal. 3: 13) and the idea of a crucified Messiah is therefore blasphemous. Gal. 1: 13f also shows a connection between his zeal for the traditions of the fathers and his persecution of Christians. In short, he attacked Christians not so much for being Christians, as for being bad Jews.

Presumably Gentile Christians would have bothered him hardly at all. Palestine was plural religiously as well as racially and culturally, and it would have been absurd and impossible for Paul to attack people because they were not Jews. It was only those whom he could regard as traitors that he could persecute. Of course some early Palestinian Christians were not regarded as traitors, people like James who faithfully kept the Law (see the consistent picture in Acts, Gal. 2, and the witness of Josephus and Eusebius, Jewish and Christian historians respectively). It is often held that others were less committed to the Law, such as Stephen and the other 'Hellenists' of Acts 6–7 (see especially the charges in 6: 11–14). If so, then most probably it was Christians of this sort that Paul persecuted, cf. Acts 7: 58.

On several occasions he tells us that what led him to such a radical change of mind and become, not the sort of Christian who stayed faithful to the Law, but one whose gospel was at least relatively Law-free, was an encounter with Christ himself.

'Have I not seen Jesus our Lord?' (1 Cor. 9: 1)

'Last of all, as to one untimely born, he appeared also to me. For I am the least of the apostles, unfit to be called an apostle, because I persecuted the church of God.' (1 Cor. 15: 8f)

'. . . when he who had set me apart before I was born, and had called me through his grace, was pleased to reveal his Son to me, in order that I might preach him among the Gentiles . . .' (Gal. 1: 15f)

Now three times, Chaps. 9, 22, 26, Acts tells the story of his 'conversion' on the road to Damascus and the facts that these accounts do not exactly tally either with each other or with what Paul himself says, suggest that it was a well-known story existing in more than one version. Unlike the author of Acts (26: 19), Paul is sure that he had no vision, but a veritable meeting with the risen Christ, and that this enabled him to be an apostle (1 Cor. 9: 1). Moreover, it constituted his call, a better word than 'conversion', for he did not regard himself as having left one religion for another. Christianity is not a new tree, but an old one, in full continuity with Israel's past (Rom. 11); new Gentile Christian branches are grafted in, while old and unproductive ones are removed in pruning, but the tree goes on. So, Jews who fail to respond to Christ as the true seed of Abraham are no longer truly Israel (see also Rom. 4 and Gal. 3). Christianity is not a new religion, but the fulfilment of the old. We should thus speak of a conversion only in the sense that, having been an opponent of Jesus, he now became his servant. He himself speaks of his 'call'.

His call was not simply to be a follower of Christ, but to be an apostle to the Gentiles. In itself this may not seem remarkable; after all Acts shows Peter responding to the need of the Gentile Cornelius and receiving him into the Christian community under divine compulsion. Did Paul simply join an existing Gentile mission like that perhaps implied in Acts 8? We know almost nothing about such an early mission, but two things require us to stress rather than play down Paul's role in opening the church to the Gentiles. First, for him it was not just a matter of gathering Gentiles into a Jewish fold, which no Jewish Christian was likely to resist. Rather, it became a major enterprise in its own right, indeed for the time being *the* major enterprise (see Rom. 9–11), of more significance in the middle term than the Jewish mission, though in the end 'all Israel will be saved' (Rom. 11: 26). Secondly, his conception of the Gentile mission entailed incorporating Gentiles into the people of God without first requiring their submission to the Law, even in such basic matters as undergoing circumcision. The only entrance requirement was faith, and pagan converts need not and must not accept Israel's legal obligations. If they do, the sufficiency of Christ for human salvation is endangered. This understanding of his mission, and of what is required of a convert, must be what he means in Gal. 1: 12 when he says that his gospel was not taught him by men, as we have already noted.

We shall take up in Chapters 4 and 6 some of the repercusssions of this understanding of his call, especially in relation to Israel as the people of God and to the Law. We now simply observe that becoming a Christian, being given a mission to the Gentiles, and coming to a radical view about what was (and was not) required of Gentile entrants to the people of God, are all connected by Paul to his meeting with Jesus Christ. In short that meeting was or became crucial not only for his discipleship, but also for his theology. Once again, he did not become the sort of Christian who added belief in the messiahship of Jesus to observance of the Law and to Temple-devotion. He so changed his angle of vision that what had once been central for him now became peripheral: 'Neither circumcision counts for anything, nor uncircumcision, but a new creation' (Gal. 6: 15).

It is because all his theological concerns arise from this shift of centre that we shall begin with his Christology (his understanding of the nature and work of Jesus Christ). This is not the only possible starting-point. Some studies take as a framework his doctrine of salvation (in the past, the present, and the future). Some, especially in the tradition of the Reformation, take justification by faith as the central and controlling factor. Some have thought his theology to be essentially anthropology, concerned with authentic and inauthentic ways of being human. Others find the centre to be his idea of a new being in Christ. Undoubtedly a strong case can be made for each, for each represents something important, and it is hard to determine what the true centre of Pauline thought is. Indeed it is not self-evident that there is a centre, especially when there is such disagreement about its location. One reason for starting with Christology is that it is where Paul himself started; this was the change at the centre from which all the other changes flowed. Paul did not adopt a system; he entered into service to a Lord, a Lord who not only conveyed God's revelation to the world but was that revelation. The shocking thing about it, especially to a Jew, was that he had none the less been rejected by his own people and crucified, not at all the kind of revelation we might expect. Yet for Paul he is the key to reality, despite having incurred the Law's curse. So how can he account for this, and how describe him?

Who is Jesus? — The Bringer of the End

One obvious thing was to call him the Messiah (literally 'the anointed one', 'Christ' in Greek). It is disputed whether Jesus ever claimed messiahship for himself, but certainly his followers quickly claimed it for him. They saw him as the Messiah, though in itself this does not tell us very much. It seems clear that by no means all Jewish circles looked for an anointed figure in whom the fulfilment of God's purposes would be focused. There were some who looked for more than one Messiah, as at Qumran where the hope was for a priestly Messiah and also for a kingly one. There were some who looked for a fulfilment figure to whom some other title was given, or one whose functions would be other than Davidic and kingly. Some hoped for an otherworldly figure, not usually called a Messiah. If we none the less suspect that many people did await a Messiah whose functions would be political, nationalistic, and even military, then such associations were not taken over either by Paul or by the generality of early Christians. Even when they referred to Jesus as Son of David (e.g. Rom. 1: 3), they seem in fact not to have regarded his functions as like those of King David. Paul, indeed, makes surprisingly little of the messiahship of Jesus, though he certainly believes in it. He regularly uses the title as little more than a name, with no stress on its meaning; there are few places where he says anything of theological importance about it (exceptions are Rom. 1: 3, where he is probably quoting traditional material, and Rom. 9: 5). The reason for this relative silence is not hard to find. Even in Palestine, the sense in which Jesus was proclaimed as Messiah was complicated and in need of explanation. Outside Jewish circles it would have been a cause of embarrassment or else quite unintelligible. Few would have known what a Messiah was, and therefore could not be expected to respond to the message that Jesus was he. Those few who knew, might well have thought of a revolutionary political figure of the Fidel Castro type, and therefore have taken it for granted that Christianity was a movement of political subversion. This might win friends in Palestine, but would alienate potential Gentile converts and invite the hostile attentions of the Roman state.

If it said too much of a dangerous sort in one direction, it said too little in another, for it was an essentially human title. The Messiah would be God's agent, raised up by him, but still a human figure. Paul, however, wanted to say more than human things about Jesus, just as he wanted to say more than Jewish things about him. In other words, Jesus was much more than Messiah; he was Lord.

Nevertheless Paul goes on using the term, and it is interesting that he does so in two main ways. First, it occurs perfunctorily (Jesus Christ, or Christ Jesus) almost as a second name without any explicit content. Secondly, it occurs in connection with faith-participation in the saving death and resurrection of Jesus. In such contexts the term 'Lord' does not occur, but 'Jesus', 'Jesus Christ', or 'Christ' (see, for example, Rom. 6: 1–11; 1 Cor. 15: 1–5, 12–19). Similarly, believers who belong to the saved community are 'in Christ' (e.g. 1 Cor. 15: 22). This suggests that the sort of Christ (Messiah) in whom Paul believes is essentially a rejected, crucified, and then divinely vindicated one, in whose death and new life those who believe in him may share. This, and not in any conventionally messianic way, is how Paul sees him.

We may wonder why he uses the title at all. Why not simply ignore it and opt for more immediately appropriate ones like 'Lord'? To a considerable extent he does just that, but he also goes on using 'Christ' probably to underline the fact that Jesus is a *fulfilment* figure. The Messiah was commonly believed to mark the end of the old age and the dawn — or at least the promise of the dawn — of the New Age. It is true that in apocalyptic schemes the figure of a Messiah was far from invariably present; it really fitted more naturally into the older, more nationalistic hope, than into the cosmic apocalyptic one. Yet the mixture did occur in Qumran, in the somewhat later 2 (IV) Esdras, and of course in Paul's writings. So, the fact that Jesus is the Christ means that the last days are upon the world; his rising from the dead is the beginning (the first-fruits, see 1 Cor. 15: 23) of the general resurrection and so the beginning of the End.

Yet it was apparent that the End had not come. The world as a whole went on as before with its sin and hostility to God, its oppression of the righteous, and its preoccupation with the temporary rather than the eternal. The End is here, because of Jesus the Christ, but it is also not here. This anomaly was not altogether new: the idea of a period between the coming of the Messiah and the general resurrection to judgment was not unknown in Judaism (it is found, for instance, in 2 (IV) Esdras). Paul solved the problem by accepting from Christian tradition the idea of a further coming of Jesus, this time in inescapable glory, often referred to as the *parousia* (Greek for 'presence' or 'coming'). See for example 1 Thess. 4: 13–18; 1 Cor. 15: 20–28. The same Jesus Christ who died and rose again will be the Judge at the End (2 Cor. 5: 10, though in Rom. 14: 10 it is God who will be Judge), will gather together those who belong to him, and will finally hand over power and authority to the Father (1 Cor. 15: 23–5).

Paul can also speak of the End without specifying Christ's *parousia* as part of it, as in Rom. 13: 11f. It is a matter of debate how far he thought the End was very near, a question raised by the same passage. Did he change his mind on the subject, originally expecting to live to see the End, but eventually, perhaps after some particularly harrowing experience, expecting to die before it? The indications are not all in one direction, though it is broadly true that in his earliest letter, 1 Thessalonians, his expectation of the End is more dominant and more urgent than in later letters like Romans (in Colossians and Ephesians it is very muted indeed, though not entirely absent, see Col. 3: 4). In Philippians, which could be either later than Romans, or as much as a decade earlier, he faces the possibility of death before the *parousia* in 1: 21–3, yet in 2: 16, 3: 20f, and 4: 5, he seems to expect to share the great event with his readers. It is impossible to be sure what change there was in his expectation.

We have already said that he saw the resurrection of Christ as the beginning of the resurrection of believers (1 Cor. 15: 23). What this means we must discuss in Chapter 5, but meanwhile must refer to the problem of believers who die before the *parousia*. That it was a problem shows that the original expectation must have been for a very early coming. When people began to die before the End, there was need for some reassurance that they would not thereby miss out, and so in 1 Thess. 4: 13–18 we find the answer suggested that the surviving believers and those who have died will simultaneously meet the Lord in the clouds (there is an echo of this solution in 1 Cor. 15: 51). Nevertheless the underlying assumption remains that the End will occur within the lifetime of many of the present generation.

It would be a mistake to make too much of this rather confused matter. Paul spends the greater part of his effort in working out the implications of what has happened, not of what will happen. His readers are those 'upon whom the end of the ages has come' (1 Cor. 10: 11). Christ's resurrection has taken place, and the Spirit has been given. The decisive eschatological events, though not of course all of them, have already occurred. There may be questions about the how (1 Cor. 15) and the when (1 Thess. 4) of the resurrection of believers, but no uncertainty about the fact. There may be dispute about the manifestations of the Spirit (1 Cor. 14), but no doubt that his presence is the sign of the activity of the powers of the new age (Joel 2: 28f). We shall see again and again that Paul writes within the framework of the two ages, which are reflected in the two sorts of power under which people may live: see below on the People of the Future (Chap. 4), on Salvation (Chap. 5) and on Ethics and the Nearness of the End and Ethics in the New Age (Chap. 6).

Jesus as Messiah is the key figure of the End of human history, who reveals and embodies the whole pattern and purpose of God's dealings with the world. All the past has been or will be fulfilled in him, for he is the key to salvation. Since apocalyptic commonly took a cosmic rather than a strictly nationalistic view of the coming age, it may cause little surprise that Paul sees the eschatological significance of Jesus as embracing Gentiles as well as Jews. Yet there is a difference: for Paul, as not for apocalyptic generally, God cares for Jews and Gentiles equally. The Jew is first chronologically (Rom. 1: 16), but in importance to God there is no distinction (Gal. 3: 28).

Who is Jesus? — Wisdom

As a messianic fulfilment-figure, Jesus is the key to God's eternal purpose for the world. Therefore, when facing people who believe they have peculiar insight or wisdom (whether or not they are Gnostics), Paul in 1 Cor. 1–4 insists that true wisdom is to be found in Christ alone. He is both the wisdom of God and the revelation of the mystery of God.

Wisdom (Greek *sophia*) was a common Gnostic motif, but was also prized in Hellenistic circles with no particular philosophical pretensions, and in Judaism (see the volume in this series by J. Blenkinsopp, *Wisdom and Law*). It is the Jewish use that is now usually believed to be the key to Paul's use. As early as the book of Proverbs, 'wisdom' was apt to be more than an attribute of God which mankind may or may not also possess. Rather, it was a way of talking about the divine activity without descending into anthropomorphism and so reducing God to human dimensions. It is tempting to say that wisdom was regarded as an entity existing alongside God, but it is unlikely that anything more than figurative personification was meant. Thus we read in Prov. 8: 22f, 29b–30: ('Wisdom' is speaking)

'The Lord created me at the beginning of his work,
   the first of his acts of old.
Ages ago I was set up,
   at the first, before the beginning of the earth . . .
. . . when he marked out the foundations of the earth,
   then I was beside him, like a master workman;
and I was daily his delight,
   rejoicing before him always . . . (cf. Job 28)

Later writings see a development of this description of wisdom's role in relation to God. In Ecclesiasticus, wisdom comes down to earth from God in order to find a dwelling, but among all the nations only Israel welcomes her. Consequently only in Israel is God's truth to be heard and known. Indeed, wisdom is identified with the Torah, for it is in the Torah that knowledge of God is found (Ecclus. 24: 23).

In some Jewish circles wisdom ideas went even further. In the Hellenistic Jewish Wisdom of Solomon, wisdom appears virtually as another heavenly being derived from God and existing beside him, his agent in creation and also — for those willing to receive her — his agent in revelation (Chaps. 7 and 8). In 1 Enoch 42, wisdom comes from God to reveal his truth, but is rejected and returns to heaven, though 42: 3 suggests she is received by a select few. Philo, using *Logos* ('Word') rather than *Sophia*, gives a similar picture. It is worth repeating that this story about wisdom was probably not taken literally; it was a way of describing God's activity without anthropomorphism and without infringing monotheism. Increasingly it is being perceived that in general and sometimes in detail, this story underlies much New Testament thought about Jesus, as in the Christ-hymns of Phil. 2: 6–11 and Col. 1: 15–20, as in John 1: 1–18, and as in many scattered statements.

In 1 Cor. 1–4 Paul opposes an undefined 'worldly wisdom'. Whatever it is, Paul replies that true wisdom is found only in Christ (1 Cor. 1: 20, 27; 2: 5, 13; 3: 18–20) and that those who are proud of their wisdom are fools in God's sight. Yet he goes further, and says that Christ not merely reveals God's wisdom, he *is* that wisdom (1 Cor. 1: 24): '. . . to those who are called, both Jews and Greeks, Christ the power of God and the wisdom of God.' This secret and hidden wisdom which was with God from the beginning (1 Cor. 2: 7) is thus revealed not only in the activity but also in the person of Christ. The identification of Christ with wisdom may well be one of the crucial things that leads Paul to talk of him in more than human terms: Christ was with the Father from the beginning, and was sent by the Father to reveal him and to redeem humanity, and after being rejected, returned to the Father. The identification is found in 1 Cor. 8: 5f, and also in Rom. 11: 36: 'For from him and through him and to him are all things', cf. v. 33. Now it is not an abstract wisdom-figure who focuses the activity of God, but the concrete figure of Jesus Christ.

1 Cor. 2: 7 says there is something hidden and mysterious about Christ as the wisdom of God. This does not mean something esoteric and accessible only to a gifted few, but rather that God's eternal purpose which has hitherto been concealed from the world has now been revealed to all who are willing to see and receive it. Its hiddenness thus belongs to apocalyptic and not to mystery religion circles of thought (cf. Dan. 12; 2 (IV) Esdr. 14). 'Mystery' (Greek *mustērion*) can mean something difficult to understand, especially something concerning God (Rom. 11: 25; 1 Cor. 13: 2; 14: 2). Often, however, it means the divine purpose now brought to light in Jesus Christ, as in Rom. 16: 25f. Because Christ embodies that eternal purpose, he can be called the 'mystery', as in some manuscripts of 1 Cor. 2: 1 and as in 1 Cor. 2: 7, where Paul's statement translates literally as 'we speak of a wisdom of

God in a mystery, hidden, which God foreknew before the ages for our glory'. Sometimes it is the whole Christian story that is called a mystery, or mysteries, once again not because it is esoteric, but because it is only now that it has become accessible (1 Cor. 4: 1; 15: 51). The identification of Christ as the mystery is sharper in Colossians (1: 26f; 2: 2; 4: 3), though not in Ephesians where the mystery appears to be the unity of Gentile and Jew in the church and in Christ (3: 3f, 9; perhaps 6: 19, but contrast 1: 9).

Wisdom and mystery are closely connected conceptions and are in fact juxtaposed in 1 Cor. 2: 7 (cf. Col. 1: 26–8; 2: 2f). Both take Jesus Christ as the crucial event in God's dealings with the world, the centre point, the critical disclosure and action. Although their associations are quite different from those of 'Messiah', they too are models or paradigms used to convey the centrality and finality of Jesus.

Who is Jesus? — Lord

Kurios ('Lord') is the most frequent and the most important way of referring to Jesus in the Pauline letters. The confession 'Jesus is Lord' is the distinguishing mark of a Christian (Rom. 10: 9; 1 Cor. 12: 3). What did Paul mean by it, and where did he get it from?

We may begin by looking at 1 Cor. 8: 5f: 'For although there may be so-called gods in heaven or on earth — as indeed there are many "gods" and many "lords" — yet for us there is one God, the Father, from whom are all things and for whom we exist, and one Lord, Jesus Christ, through whom are all things and through whom we exist.' God and Lord are not identical, but are related much as Yahweh and wisdom are in some of the passages discussed in the previous section. All things are *from*, that is originating in, deriving out of, the Father, but *through* the Son, that is by his agency. He plays the part of wisdom, and indeed this passage is to be included among those which give Christ a wisdom role. However, it also gives him the title of lordship, and does it explicitly in the light of pagan ascriptions of lordship. Clearly Paul has in mind the deities and cult figures of pagan religions including the mystery religions, who were customarily called 'lords'. Jesus thus appears as the Christians' answer to these many lords, just as God the Father is their answer to the many gods. The passage comes in the context of the problem of Christians' relationship to pagan cult meals. He states, more or less in parenthesis, that of course there are many divinities and lords in the world, but does not necessarily mean that they really exist. His point is that they exist for the people who acknowledge and serve them and he is not concerned with the ultimate question, though judging by v. 4 he would deny their real existence. Moreover, though in paganism it was not unusual to worship more than one god or to participate in more than one cult, such plurality was impossible for Christians. In the Jewish tradition they are monotheists: there is only God the Father from whom all creation is derived.

Now whether or not paganism distinguished between gods and lords, Paul does. Jesus is Lord, the Father is God. This is not to undervalue the Lord, but to make it clear that he is the agent both of creation ('through whom are all things') and of redemption ('through whom we exist', 'we' probably meaning the Christian believers). In this passage 'Lord' thus stands in close association with 'God', but is not identical with it. Further, the use of 'Lord' in this quite explicit comparison with paganism shows that Paul is thinking of one to whom the Christians belonged, one whom they served, and one who gave shape, significance, and a centre to their lives. Thus, though these verses inevitably raise questions about the relation between Father and Lord, their primary purpose is to contrast pagan belonging with Christian belonging, and to assert Christ's relation to believers rather than his relation to God. Nevertheless 'lord' in this pagan context certainly had divine associations, and it has often been argued that this is where ascribing lordship to Jesus began, in a Hellenistic environment. It has been thought unlikely that such ascription could have occurred in a Jewish setting, where only Yahweh could be the Lord. In the Hellenistic world, however, where divinity was not indivisible and where there could be greater or lesser degrees of it, ascribing divine honours to Jesus would be easier. There is sense in the argument. Undoubtedly the ascription could be made more readily in such circles, especially as the divine claims of Roman emperors arose. They came to insist on being regarded as universal lords, and eventually to declare 'Caesar is lord' became a requirement of good citizenship and political loyalty, but this was after Paul's lifetime.

If this 'Hellenistic' view of the origin of the title 'Lord' is correct, two important things follow. First, it must be a relatively late development, after the church had moved out of its Jewish Palestinian womb, though it is already taken for granted in Paul's earliest letter (1 Thess. 1: 1 and often). Secondly, though it connoted divinity, it could mean divinity in a somewhat reduced sense, and would not necessarily say anything unique or even highly unusual about Jesus.

Against this theory, other scholars have argued for a Jewish and Palestinian provenance. A major part of their case is 1 Cor. 16: 22 which literally translated runs: 'If anyone does not love the Lord, let him be anathema. Marana tha.' *Marana tha* is Aramaic and probably means 'Our lord, come.' Why does Paul use an Aramaic phrase to Christians in Corinth who almost certainly knew not a word of the language? The answer commonly given is that this expression, like a very few other Aramaic words, most notably *Amen*, had become so familiar through liturgical use especially in the eucharist, that it was common coinage even in the Greek-speaking church. This argues for its considerable antiquity and its origin in the early Jerusalem church. It shows that Aramaic-speaking Christians addressed Jesus as 'Lord' from an early time. The suggestion that 'Lord' refers not to Jesus but to Yahweh has little plausibility in view of the request 'Come' and in view of the clear reference to Jesus in the parallel invocation in Rev. 22: 20: 'Amen. Come Lord Jesus.' Moreover the context in 1 Cor. 16 points to Jesus as the one addressed.

The fact that it is an invocation and not an acclamation, a request to come and be Lord, not a recognition that he is already Lord, has led to the proposal that the early Palestinian church called on him to come and be Lord, but the Hellenistic church first acclaimed him as one who reigns already. In this case, 1 Cor. 16: 22

represents the older Palestinian stage, and 1 Cor. 8: 5f the later Hellenistic one where Christ reigns in heaven with God, sharing his functions but remaining subordinate to him.

Yet this distinction is difficult. First, both passages quoted are from the same rather early letter and Paul himself seems unaware of any incongruity or development, which development must in any case have happened so swiftly that 'early' and 'later' become almost meaningless. Secondly, in an apocalyptic scheme, realities which God intends are commonly regarded as already existing in heaven with him; this means that if God intends Christ to return and be Lord, he is in effect Lord already. Invocation of a future Lord implies the acclamation of a present one. Thirdly, the widespread use of Ps. 110: 1 must be taken into account: 'The Lord says to my lord: "Sit at my right hand, till I make your enemies your footstool." ' This is frequently quoted or alluded to in the New Testament, by Paul most clearly in 1 Cor. 15: 25: 'For he must reign until he has put all his enemies under his feet.' In the psalm the first 'Lord' is clearly Yahweh, and the second when it is quoted is taken to be Jesus, so that it becomes an affirmation of the present reign of Christ which is, however, incomplete until consummated by God. This confirms the relation between invocation and acclamation already suggested, and the psalm's widespread use in quite independent writings implies its early currency (see, among many instances, Mark 12: 36; Acts 2: 34; Heb. 1: 13). If there was a development, it happened before Paul's time. For him, Christ is both present and future Lord.

In recent years, the view that Jesus even during his lifetime was not only addressed but also described as Lord has gained ground. Even if we discount the vocative *kurie* (equivalent to the polite 'sir' in English), it is likely that as a charismatic, wonder-working, and Rabbi-like figure he was regarded as Lord. This would not have been in any divine or quasi-divine sense, yet it provides a starting-point. The Aramaic equivalent *mar* we now know to have been applicable to both divine and revered human figures.

The more we examine how the use of 'Lord' developed, the more important it is to understand what such lordship meant, both in relation to the people over whom it was exercised, and in relation to the one Lord, Yahweh. A point that has often mistakenly been made is that, because in the Septuagint *kurios* was the Greek replacement of the sacred name *YHWH* which was never spoken, *Adhonai* being said instead, therefore when early Christians called Jesus *kurios*, Lord, they were granting him the same status as Yahweh. If pressed, this argument proves too much, suggesting that Jesus was Yahweh, an equation never entertained in the early church. Moreover, it now seems that *kurios* replaced *YHWH* only in Christian copies of the Septuagint, for the few fragments we possess of Jewish copies put *YHWH* into its rough equivalent in Greek characters and do not use *kurios* for the purpose. That leaves the question of what a reader in a Greek-speaking synagogue actually said, and he may well have said *kurios* because he would not utter the sacred name, and would need some Greek replacement. Moreover, Paul himself writes *kurios* in Old Testament quotations while reserving it for Jesus when he is not quoting. Yet to say that he can use the same title for both God and Jesus, without thereby equating the two, is to restate the problem, not solve it.

It is more significant that he can transfer Old Testament passages from Yahweh to Jesus. For example, in Rom. 10: 13 ' "every one who calls upon the name of the Lord will be saved" ' is widely taken to be an instance of the transfer (in Joel 2: 32 the Lord is Yahweh). We may also compare Phil. 2: 10f with Isa. 45: 23 where the reference is similarly altered to Christ from Yahweh. There is at least a close association between the two figures, but in fact they are never identified (see again 1 Cor. 8: 5f). In 1 Cor. 15: 24, 28, Christ at the End hands over the kingdom to the Father, and the final subjection of all things to God includes the subjection of Christ himself. It is such passages that lend force to the often-quoted words of L. Cerfaux that 'Christ is Lord because he is God's vice-regent, exercising a power that belongs to God.' This seems to be exactly right. God's powers and reign are exercised through Christ as God's plenipotentiary representative, but Christ is not identical with God. Things traditionally said about God may now be properly said about Christ, but not that he *is* God, for the element of subordination remains. Of course, the church could not for long be satisfied with seeing him as simply carrying out the functions of God, and it was inevitable that questions should arise about his nature, yet in Paul's thinking the focus was still firmly on Christ's functions as God's vice-regent.

'Lord' means one who has authority, and is a relational term. Authority must be concrete, exercised over someone or something. Christ's lordship is exercised over individuals, the church, and the whole cosmos including supernatural powers. The confession 'Jesus is Lord' is an individual matter, and undoubtedly for Paul to be a Christian is to acknowledge him as one's own Lord, with all life under his sovereignty. That sovereignty is established at his resurrection or exaltation, see Rom. 10: 9; Phil. 2: 9. It is the risen Christ who is Lord. Further, he is Lord of the church, binding his subjects into a unity, as we see in Rom. 14: 1–9, where in dealing with the practical matter of whether or not to eat meat, observe certain days, and drink wine, Paul repeatedly stresses that each person is under the Lord and must be faithful to him. Yet he centres the whole discussion on Christ's lordship over the church corporately; its members must live together in a responsible way under him. Again, although Christ's lordship over himself is often acknowledged when he begins letters with the self-description 'servant/slave of Jesus Christ' (Phil. 1: 1; Rom. 1: 1; cf. 2 Cor. 4: 5), the corporate nature of that lordship is expressed when he commands his readers to do something 'in the Lord' (e.g. Phil. 4: 2, 4, and cf. Col. 2: 6).

This lordship is also cosmic and universal. This is especially evident in the later Pauline or even post-Pauline Colossians and Ephesians, see especially Col. 1: 15–20 and Eph. 1: 19–23, where we find a crescendo of acclamation of Christ as Lord over all authorities and powers in heaven and on earth. If he is God's vice-regent, he is vice-regent over everything. Yet this thinking is not confined to these later letters, for in a less elaborated but unmistakable form it occurs in letters agreed to be early and genuine. It is found in 1 Cor. 8: 6, where Christ is he through whom all things exist, the mediator of all creation. Moreover, Christ is head of the supernatural powers, so that believers are freed from their control. This lies behind Rom. 8: 38f: 'I am sure that neither death, nor life, nor angels, nor principalities, nor things present, nor things to come, nor powers, nor height, nor depth, nor anything else in all creation, will be able to separate us from the love of God in Christ Jesus our Lord' (cf. Col. 1: 20; perhaps Gal. 4: 3). However, although 'Christ died and lived again, that he might be Lord both of the dead and of the living' (Rom. 14: 9), this victory will not be complete until the End, cf. 1 Cor. 15: 24ff. Yet even though his reign is not consummated in the meantime, it does already give him a cosmic position, and undoubtedly we are moving firmly away from a merely human Jesus.

Who is Jesus? — Son of God

Compared with 'Lord', this title is used by Paul infrequently, but see Rom. 1: 3f, 9; 1 Cor. 1: 9 as examples. By the Second Century, it came to refer to Jesus Christ as divine, but originally it was not a particularly lofty title. It is not the same as God the Son, the Second Person of the Trinity. Though it was not particularly common, it could be used of human beings, both in the Jewish and in the Greek world.

In Old Testament tradition, Israel was God's son, as in Hos. 11: 1: 'Out of Egypt have I called my son.' See also Exod. 4: 22; Isa. 43: 6 etc. As the nation's representative, the king was God's son, as in 2 Sam. 7: 14; Ps. 2: 7. Angels (Gen. 6: 2, 4; Deut. 32: 8) were sons of God, as were in later times outstandingly righteous men (Wisd. 2: 10–20; 5: 1–5). There is little evidence that the Messiah was so entitled, though there may be an instance in the Dead Sea Scrolls, but as the new and greater David it would have been natural to describe him so (and see Matt. 16: 16).

Such ascriptions did not mean that the nation or the king or the righteous man was genetically related to God. Israel rejected any idea of that. Rather, being Son of God meant obedient service to God on the one hand, and divine commissioning and endorsement on the other. In our society we tend to forget that the first thing about a son was that he obeyed his father; therefore calling

Jesus Christ Son of God meant first of all that he did what God wanted. He was the obedient one.

In the Hellenistic world the title could be given to particularly powerful and charismatic people: kings, philosophers, heroes, miracle-workers; any who demonstrated the presence in them of extraordinary and therefore presumably supernatural powers. From Augustus onwards, Roman emperors were regarded as gods, at first mostly in the Eastern Empire, but eventually in Rome too, and even in their own lifetime. We recall that in some Hellenistic circles the gulf between gods and men was not as great as the gulf between Yahweh and humanity in Judaism, and the conception of a demi-god, half man and half god, was possible. No doubt, while the simple took such language literally, the more educated often took it with a pinch of salt or at best metaphorically, but at least such figures were not unfamiliar. To call Jesus Son of God in such circles was not necessarily to say anything very exalted. Perhaps this is why Paul refers to Christ as *the* Son of God (1 Cor. 15: 28; 2 Cor. 1: 19) or as his *own* Son (Rom. 8: 3) or simply as *his* Son (Gal. 4: 4).

Paul's use of the title reflects the Jewish rather than the pagan background. He uses it to convey Christ's carrying out the divine purposes: he is given up by God for our sake (Rom. 8: 32; Gal. 2: 20); his death reconciles us to God (Rom. 5: 10; cf. Col. 1: 13f); indeed all God's promises are accomplished through him (2 Cor. 1: 19f). Not surprisingly, the resurrection is the crucial moment of his becoming the Son, whether it is when his sonship begins, or when it is confirmed and made evident. Much interpretation of Rom. 1: 3f revolves around this question, because the word translated in RSV as 'designated' can bear either meaning. The discussion is complicated by the probability that Paul is quoting a traditional formula, whose Christology was not necessarily in all details the same as his. It is even sometimes suggested that originally Paul expected Jesus to become Son of God at the *parousia*, 1 Thess. 1: 9f, but this relies too much on one ambiguous passage.

Different passages seem to point to different moments of becoming the Son. Some may even point to his existing as an individual before his birth: Phil. 2: 6–11 can be so read, and the use of Wisdom language may imply it, depending on how literally it was taken. Certainly it implies that the divine purposes fulfilled in Christ were pre-existent, but not necessarily that he himself was. That God *sent* Christ (Gal. 4: 4f; Rom. 8: 3) as the Son does not in itself mean his pre-existence, for the prophets are also sent (Isa. 6: 8; Jer. 1: 6; Ezek. 2: 3) and so are Moses, Aaron, and Miriam (Mic. 6: 4). 'Sending' language rather underlines the Son's commissioning, obedience, and special relationship to God.

In short, it is impossible to be dogmatic about when Paul sees Christ becoming the Son. One thing that is clear is that Christ's sonship makes possible the sonship of those who believe in him: 'But when the time had fully come, God sent forth his Son, born of woman, born under the law, to redeem those who were under the law, so that we might receive adoption as sons . . .' (Gal. 4: 4f). Although obedience is a leading note here, so also is a relation of intimacy: 'And because you are sons, God has sent the Spirit of his Son into our hearts, crying, "Abba! Father!" So through God you are no longer a slave but a son, and if a son then an heir.' (Gal. 4: 6f; see also Rom. 8: 14ff, and compare Rom. 8: 29; 9: 26; 2 Cor. 6: 18; Gal. 3: 26). 'Abba', found in the New Testament only here, in Rom. 8: 15, and in the Gethsemane episode in Mark 14: 36, points to something like the relationship of an earthly child to its father, for it is the intimate family word rather than the solemn liturgical one. Its use may be not as unprecedented as was once thought, but it does seem to have been unusual, and suggests that the close relationship to God that Christ enjoyed is now, according to Paul, available through him to his followers. This role of enabling others to be sons marks him out as unique.

A hymn to Christ as Lord

In facing the question of the relation of Christ to Yahweh we must not outrun the evidence and read into Paul's language the Fourth Century definition of Christ as God the Son, co-equal and co-eternal, of one substance with the Father. Paul's language is one of the factors leading to that definition, and also part of the problem it attempted to solve, but it would be anachronistic to interpret his language in such later terms. Perhaps he preferred 'Lord' as a title because of its ambiguity, because it established Christ's relation to humanity, church, and cosmos, without too closely defining his relation to Yahweh. As a Jewish monotheist Paul would wish neither to be accused of believing in two Gods, nor of claiming that Yahweh died on the cross. The only place in the undisputed letters where he may equate Christ with God is Rom. 9: 5 if a full stop is not placed after 'Christ', so that it reads '. . . of their race . . . is the Christ who is God over all . . .'. More probably it should read '. . . of their race . . . is the Christ. God who is over all be blessed . . . '. More certain is the fact that for Paul 'God was in Christ, reconciling the world to himself' (2 Cor. 5: 19). This accurately reflects Paul's belief that Christ's activity conveys God's activity, and that what Christ *does* is what matters.

Many of these issues are focused in the 'Christ-hymn' of Phil. 2: 6–11:

> . . . though he was in the form of God, [he] did not count equality with God a thing to be grasped, but emptied himself, taking the form of a servant, being born in the likeness of men. And being found in human form he humbled himself and became obedient unto death, even death on a cross. Therefore God has highly exalted him and bestowed on him the name which is above every name, that at the name of Jesus every knee should bow, in heaven and on earth and under the earth, and every tongue confess that Jesus Christ is Lord, to the glory of God the Father.

Because of its condensed and memorable form, more obvious in Greek than in translation, this is widely believed to be a piece of early liturgical tradition that Paul is quoting. It falls into two stanzas, vv. 6–8 describing Christ's humiliation, and vv. 9–11 describing his exaltation. In one or two places Paul may have expanded it, especially by adding in v. 8 'even death on a cross'.

Paul's reason for quoting it is to commend an attitude especially within the church (v. 5) of caring for others rather than being arrogant or self-seeking, but Christ offers not so much an example to be followed, as a pattern of life and a lordship to be entered. Thus the hymn concludes not with advice about how to live, but with an acclamation of Christ as Lord, under whom believers live.

Although the main thrust is clear, many details of the hymn are anything but clear to us, and the background of thought is equally uncertain. Possibly a Gnostic Redeemer myth is the framework, so that Christ is portrayed as a heavenly figure who descends to carry out his mission, and then returns to his divine origins. Such a framework would suggest that the hymn is about the pre-existence, the incarnation, and the ascent of a heavenly Christ. A similar conclusion follows if a descending and ascending Wisdom story is the framework. It is possible, however, that the background is a contrast between Christ and Adam, and in what follows I suggest an interpretation of the hymn along such lines without claiming anything like finality for it. How we translate many of the expressions depends on our view of the total picture; a different view would entail quite different treatment of many details which in themselves are highly ambiguous.

Though (v. 6) Christ like Adam was in the image ('form': the words in Greek can be synonymous) of God, unlike Adam he did not regard equality with God (i.e. being like God, see Gen. 3: 5) a matter of grabbing (or perhaps a prize to be snatched). Indeed unlike Adam (v. 7) he voluntarily accepted servanthood and mortality even to the point of a humiliating death on the cross (v. 8). He obeyed God, in contrast to Adam who vaingloriously disobeyed. The humanness and circumscription that Adam endured as punishment, Christ willingly accepted. 'Emptying himself' (v. 7) would thus mean not giving away something he hitherto had, but choosing the way of humbleness and being content to be human (the word RSV renders 'being born' in v. 7 can equally well mean 'being').

All this is the subject of the first stanza. The second stanza shows that in God's purpose the way of humiliation is the way of exaltation. God freely gives Christ what Adam had tried to grab, and bestows on him 'the name above every name', the title of 'Lord' (v. 9). This lordship is universal and total. The quotation from Isa. 45: 23, 25, that at his name 'every knee should bow . . .' is another instance where a passage that in the Old Testament refers to Yahweh is by Paul referred instead to Christ, and where the divine honours that are appropriate to Yahweh are rendered to Christ. To make the point absolutely clear the quotation is expanded by the words 'in heaven and on earth and under the earth', so that nothing at all is excluded from his lordship. The ruling function that belongs properly to Yahweh alone is now Christ's also; he is cosmic Lord and as such receives the honour that hitherto has been given only to Yahweh.

Yet before we rashly conclude that the two have simply become identified, we must note that the element of subordination remains. It all happens, even the exaltation of Christ, 'to the glory of God the Father' (v. 11), and Christ does not exalt himself but is exalted by God and is given the title 'Lord' by him (v. 9). Christ has become the bearer of the powers of God and the recipient of divine homage (v. 10), but is still distinct from him and subject to him.

This conclusion about the second stanza of the hymn stands whatever view of the background of the hymn as a whole we adopt. If we had treated it against a Gnostic or a Wisdom backdrop we should have said different things about the first stanza, but substantially the same about the second.

Who is Jesus? — Jesus and the Spirit

As exalted Lord, Jesus Christ is now Spirit: 'the last Adam became a life-giving spirit' (1 Cor. 15: 45). Moreover, the Spirit is now not merely the Spirit of God, but also the Spirit of Christ. In 2 Cor. 3: 16f Paul seems to equate Christ and the Spirit: 'Now the Lord is the Spirit, and where the Spirit of the Lord is, there is freedom.' This is confusing; if the Lord *is* the Spirit, how can we also have the Spirit *of* the Lord? Probably the answer is that the first 'Lord' refers to v. 16, 'But when a man turns to the Lord the veil is removed', which is an allusion to Exod. 34: 34, and that Paul means that the Lord *in that passage* is the Holy Spirit. The second 'Lord', however, is Christ, for in v. 14 he says it is Christ who enables the veil over the old covenant to be removed. Here, then, the Spirit is defined as the Spirit of Christ (see also Rom. 8: 9, where he is both the Spirit of God and the Spirit of Christ; Phil. 1: 19).

How then can Paul in 1 Cor. 15: 45 say that the last Adam became Spirit? First of all, he means that Christ is no longer physical; this is clear from the preceding argument. It also means that Christ now communicates with the world and creates new life in his new mode of being as the Spirit. For what is the Spirit? Fundamentally Paul is in line with Old Testament thought: it is not a question of spirit, a natural component of human beings, perhaps thought of as an almost infinitely fine substance within and pervading the grosser physical substance as in one Hellenistic view, but a question of Spirit, God himself. Spirit is the mode of God's presence and power at work in the world, in other words God himself in his activity especially towards mankind. So he is the agent of life (Gen. 1: 2), and of all unusual and powerful human activity, as in the case of Samson, Judg. 13: 25. In effect, speaking of God's Spirit was a way of speaking about God's activity without descending into anthropomorphism, and it is God himself who is meant, not some additional entity or being.

According to Joel 2: 28f, in the Last Days the Spirit will be universally evident, and not just in the lives of a selected few. Christians believed those Last Days had begun, and that the Spirit was consequently at work in their midst in all sorts of ways (see especially 1 Cor. 12). In this they run parallel to the community of Qumran, for whom the coming new age was to be the age of the Spirit (1QS 4, 11; cf. Paul's use of the idea in the Hagar-Sarah allegory in Gal. 4). To live in the Spirit was thus to live in the power of the new age, and this was the opposite of ordinary life centred in this age with its goals and standards and securities.

What Paul is saying about Christ and the Spirit is therefore twofold. On the one hand, Christ is now Spirit, especially in the way he comes to his people and deals with them. He does not come as the historical person Jesus of Nazareth, but comes in the way God does, which is why Spirit of God and of Christ are equivalent in Rom. 8: 9. On the other hand, Spirit is now defined by Christ: he is not merely God's, but Christ's, and the content that fills the word is Christ-content. This does not mean that we may simply identify the Spirit and Christ, because the two are not exactly of a kind: Spirit is fundamentally a name for the divine working, and Christ is a name for an historical — though now exalted and heavenly — person. Indeed, the expression 'Spirit of Christ' makes a straightforward identification impossible.

If the Spirit and Christ are not to be confused, neither in practice from the believer's point of view can they be distinguished. Because the Spirit communicates Christ, his earthly work and his present authority, Paul can pass from one to the other almost without noticing. Christ is in us and the Spirit is in us (Rom. 8: 9f); we are in Christ and in the Spirit (Rom. 8: 1, 9); there is joy in the Spirit and in the Lord (Rom. 14: 17; Phil. 4: 4), peace in the Spirit and in the Lord (Rom. 14: 17; Phil. 4: 7) and so on. It is because the Spirit now conveys Christ and conversely since Christ now encounters mankind as the Spirit, that such sets of statements can be drawn up. Indeed it is crucial for Paul that Spirit-experience be Christ-experience, that it be anchored in the concrete person and history of Christ (see Rom. 8: 14ff; 1 Cor. 12: 3; 2 Cor. 3: 8). Christ and the Spirit in effect define one another.

Arguably, we here reach the summit of Paul's Christology with Christ firmly in the divine category. Christ, like God, encounters us as and through the Spirit. Moreover, this enables Paul to speak of Christ's present rule and functions without prolonging the resurrection period. Christ is exalted and in a sense absent, as Christ. He is present and active in lordship, however, because he is now understood and experienced as the Spirit. Yet once again it appears that Paul's primary concern is not with the definition of Christ's place in relation to the one God, but with his activity.

4

Christ and his People

Paul's understanding of Christ is not merely individualistic. Rather, Christ is the centre of a new people which is also an old people, both the fulfilment of historical Israel and the replacement of that part of contemporary Israel which rejected him (see the figure of the olive tree in Rom. 11). Before we take up the relation between church and Israel, we must first discuss one of the knottiest problems in Pauline study: the way in which Paul speaks of Christ in more than individual terms, what is sometimes called 'the corporate Christ'. This is seen in three main areas, all apparently involving some sort of participation by believers in Christ.

Corporate language: 1. 'In Christ'

He frequently speaks of Christians, individually and collectively, as being 'in Christ', 'in the Lord', 'in him'. Even if we subtract those instances where the meaning could straightforwardly be something like 'by the instrumentality of Christ' (e.g. 1 Cor. 1: 2, 'sanctified *by* Christ Jesus'?) or 'on the authority of Christ' (e.g. 1 Thess. 4: 1), and those which speak of God or his love being in Christ (e.g. Rom. 8: 39; 2 Cor. 5: 19), a large number remains. Among the most important are:

> There is neither Jew nor Greek, there is neither slave nor free, there is neither male nor female; for you are all one in Christ Jesus. (Gal. 3: 28)
> There is therefore now no condemnation for those who are in Christ Jesus. (Rom. 8: 1)
> . . . that I may gain Christ and be found in him . . . (Phil. 3: 8f).

The puzzle increases when we see that Paul can also say the converse, that Christ is in believers, e.g. Rom. 8: 10: 'But if Christ is in you, although your bodies are dead because of sin, your spirits are alive because of righteousness.' The most notable other instance is Gal. 2: 20: 'I have been crucified with Christ; it is no longer I who live, but Christ who lives in me . . .' This is the only passage where there is anything like an interchange, believers in Christ and Christ in believers, for he has just said (v. 17) that they are justified in Christ. This is, however, an insufficient basis on which to found a notion of 'mutual penetration' between Christ and believers, and anyway it is difficult to know what that could mean.

Generally, believers *exist* in Christ, but Christ is *active* in believers, and so the two notions are not exactly parallel. The acting nature of the second notion is particularly evident where 'in' is not a separate preposition but is the prefix to a verb (see Gal. 2: 8; Phil. 2: 13; cf. Col. 1: 29). Further, while Christ is usually in the believer individually, believers are often in Christ corporately, as a people, as in Gal. 3: 27f quoted above.

There appears to be little difference between being in Christ and being in the Lord, though the second tends to occur in exhortatory contexts, those giving instruction or encouragement, and the first in kerygmatic contexts, those making statements about the gospel, the *kerygma*. Thus 'in the Lord' often occurs in sentences where the verb is imperative, and 'in Christ' in sentences where it is indicative (compare Phil. 4: 2, 4 with 1 Cor. 4: 15), but the distinction cannot be pressed as it by no means invariably holds. In Rom. 16 both expressions occur very frequently, with no apparent difference in meaning.

As we should expect from what we saw at the end of the previous chapter about the relation between Christ and the Spirit, there is also little if any difference between being in Christ and being in the Spirit. The expressions appear to be interchangeable. Rom. 8 is a major source of this sort of language, and it clearly demonstrates the equivalence. In v. 1 believers are 'in Christ Jesus', and perhaps also in v. 2, but in v. 4 they walk 'according to the Spirit' and in vv. 5f 'set the mind on the Spirit', but above all are *in* the Spirit, v. 9, yet also have the Spirit in them, vv. 9, 11. We shall see that far from creating confusion, this equivalence may be one of the clues to the meaning of Paul's participatory language. Meanwhile, we can notice that there is no perceptible difference between being in the Spirit and having the Spirit in oneself.

The main difficulty in examining this language is that nowhere does Paul explain himself, but assumes that his readers will readily understand it. Indeed, he uses it to explain other things; it is needed to explain his argument against sex with a prostitute in 1 Cor. 6: 13–18, and similarly to explain his argument against combining Christian with pagan worship in 1 Cor. 10: 14–21. It also underlies Gal. 3: 14–16, which makes little sense without it. In Gal. 3: 6–9 he has argued that the true seed (descendants) of Abraham are those who have faith, and that the promise ' "In thee shall all the nations be blessed" ' (v. 8, cf. Gen. 18: 18) applies to them and not to physical descendants. They share the faith that rendered Abraham acceptable to God before the making of the covenant, and before he had any good deeds which he could offer to God. Gentiles now by their faith in Christ are thus true children of Abraham, v. 7.

In vv. 10–13 he talks about the death of Christ, who by being crucified (hanging on a tree) incurred the curse of the Law on such people (Deut 21: 23), just as people who do not obey the whole Law incur the Law's curse as Paul sees it (v. 10; cf. Deut. 27: 26). In Christ's case the curse proved ineffective, for by raising him from the dead God vindicated him. In talking about the death of Christ Paul has not changed the subject, however, and is still talking about the Gentiles and their faith, for in v. 14 he says that it happened in order that 'in Christ Jesus the blessing of Abraham might come upon the Gentiles, that we might receive the promise of the Spirit through faith.'

The point is that the promises were made (v. 16) to Abraham *and his seed*. The word 'seed' is singular, and Paul argues that it must refer to one descendant not to a multiplicity, and that one descendant is Christ. Yet the one includes the many, and by Christ he means also those who are in him, the Gentiles who have faith.

He is still talking about how they enter the people of God: like Abraham, by faith. We see from v. 14 that Christ is not just an individual, but in some sense an incorporating figure, so that what is true of him is true also of those who belong to him, who are in him. If Christ as the one true descendant is the inheritor of the promise, then so too are Gentile believers. This corporate notion is little more than alluded to, but is required to explain the course of the argument, and the conclusion that entry into God's people is neither by race nor by obedience to the Law, but by faith, and by being in Christ.

All this constitutes a puzzle. What does Paul mean by this corporate language, and how can he take it for granted that he will be understood? Before we can attempt an answer, we must look at other manifestations of this strange language.

Corporate language: 2. The two Adams

In two important passages at least, Rom. 5: 12–21 and 1 Cor. 15: 20–3, 45–9, Paul contrasts being in Christ with being in Adam. The two are parallel but contrasting figures. He calls Christ not the second, but the last Adam (1 Cor. 15: 45). Now if we can discover what being in Adam means, we shall be well on the way to discovering what being in Christ means. We look first at the relevant verses in 1 Cor. 15:

> For as by a man came death, by a man has come also the resurrection of the dead. For as in Adam all die, so also in Christ shall all be made alive. But each in his own order: Christ the first fruits, then at his coming those who belong to Christ. (vv. 21–3)

> Thus it is written, 'The first man Adam became a living being'; the last Adam became a life-giving spirit. But it is not the spiritual which is first but the physical, and then the spiritual. The first man was from the earth, a man of dust; the second man is from heaven. As was the man of dust, so are those who are of the dust; and as is the man of heaven, so are those who are of heaven. Just as we have borne the image of the man of

dust, we shall also bear the image of the man of heaven. (vv. 45-9)

One thing is obvious at first glance: Paul is talking about two different ways of being human. Christ is not merely the inaugurator of a new — or renewed — religion, but of a new humanity, a new start to the human race. Adam is the first start, Christ the new start. It is also obvious that neither figure stands in isolation: in some unexplained sense both Adam and Christ take others with them. This is true in terms of their destiny, death or life (vv. 21-3, 45), and also of their nature, or 'image' (vv. 47-9), which refers to Gen. 1: 27.

Adam and Christ are thus representative figures. Paul is not just talking about two individuals, but about human beings as a whole. Hitherto there has been only one way of being human, the Adam way: this leads inexorably to death, v. 21, and is purely natural humanity, hence 'a living being' which quotes Gen. 2: 7, and hence the 'man of dust', which quotes Gen. 2: 7a. There is no talk here of sin, unless it is implied in v. 21, 'by a man came death'. The stress is rather on the limitation, the mere ordinary humanness, of the Adam-type humanity. His point about the natural man as chronologically prior to the spiritual man, i.e. Christ as following, not preceding Adam, may be an attempt to counter current speculations about a primeval Anthropos (Man) who was fragmented by a fall, parts of whom are therefore within human beings, but who will finally be restored and reconstituted (see p. 16). On the contrary, says Paul, the new humanity is not a return to a primordial entity, but a genuinely new thing, begun by Christ. Whether or not this is the meaning of v. 46, it is clear that Paul's stress is on the new kind of humanity which belongs to Christ and which, unlike the humanity of Adam, is remarkable for life and for its spiritual (i.e. especially grounded on and empowered by God) character. It is derived from the last Adam, who has become not merely a living thing, but a source of life for others (v. 45b), and it looks forward to sharing his image (v. 49).

Undoubtedly all this illuminates the meaning of 'in Christ', for we now see it in the perspective of old and new creation and in terms of discovering true humanity. None the less 'in' is still a puzzle. If Paul meant 'belonging to' why did he not simply use the genitive, as indeed he does in v. 23? Yet what would 'belonging to Adam' mean? It would have to mean something like belonging to the Adam category, but this would still need explanation. In fact some sort of incorporative or participatory notion must be present, because the point of the argument in this chapter is that believers will rise from the dead because Christ has been raised from the dead. His resurrection means resurrection for all who are in him (vv. 18f). His is not just chronologically the first, the beginning of the general resurrection, but — despite the time gap — it entails that of believers (vv. 17, 20–3).

It seems, then, that Paul does not start from a view of Adam, and then find an answer to human dilemmas and human death in the new Adam. Rather, he starts from a belief in the resurrection of Christ and therefore of believers, and uses Adam as a foil to that. There is a strong possibility that instead of using 'in Adam' to explain 'in Christ', we ought to work the opposite way, and learn how to understand 'in Adam' when we understand 'in Christ'. All together, while 1 Cor. 15 does considerably illuminate 'in Christ', it still does not solve the problem of the preposition 'in'.

The Adam-Christ contrast is differently used in Rom. 5: 12–21, for here it is primarily the sin of Adam that is in the forefront, and death as sin's consequence, and Christ is much more the earthly, obedient-even-to-death figure than the glorified and exalted one. As in 1 Cor. 15, Adam and Christ here too are parallel and opposite figures, and both are representative of those whose destiny and nature are included in theirs. Adam is the means of death through sin and disobedience. Christ is the means of life through obedience and righteousness: 'as one man's trespass led to condemnation for all men, so one man's act of righteousness leads to acquittal and life for all men. For as by one man's disobedience many were made sinners, so by one man's obedience many will be made righteous' (vv. 18–19). Christ's act of obedience must be his death on the cross. Moreover, Adam's sin led to the universal reign of death, but Christ's effect is the reigning in life of those who belong to him. But how?

The word 'representative' may seem unwarranted here. Paul could be arguing, as later Christians did, that Adam sinned and incurred death as a punishment, passing both sin and death on to his descendants, either as some sort of genetic inheritance or contagious disease, in the case of sin, or as a punishment in the case of death. Behind this lies the idea that his descendants were seminally in Adam, and were therefore as guilty as he was. The notion of guilt for which we have no responsibility is strange, and few hold it today, but conceivably Paul did see sin as an infection which Adam let loose on the world. The real trouble with this sort of explanation is that it fails at the point of comparison with Christ. Paul is certainly not arguing for any kind of transmission, genetically or by infection, from Christ to believers in him. It therefore makes much better sense to take Adam and Christ as representatives of two sorts of humanity, especially in relation to obedience to God, and this may be confirmed by the words translated 'because' in RSV in v. 12. These words (Greek *eph' ho(i)*) have been held to be ambiguous, able to mean either 'in so far as' or 'in whom'. If they mean 'in whom', then the verse could be saying that all people sinned in Adam, though it is hard to say what that would mean (seminally, 'in his loins'?). However it is virtually certain that RSV is right, that the Greek words mean 'in so far as' or 'because', and that Paul is saying that in fact all people sin, so that Adam is Everyman in the sense that he represents all who by sin and disobedience incur death.

Sin and death cannot be separated. Paul uses them almost interchangeably, perhaps because one inevitably results in the other, or perhaps because sin means death in relation to God. Indeed we cannot be sure how far he means physical death or 'spiritual' death (as in Rom. 8: 10) or both together, so that sin in effect *is* death-in-life, with the awful threat that it will one day be made absolute. At all events by Adam's sin we are dead, not by some infection or transmission, but arising from Adam's role as Everyman. He is not just someone who lived long ago; he is everyone, and his bondage to sin and death is the bondage of everyone. Nevertheless, because of the new Adam, 'If, because of one man's trespass, death reigned through that one man, much more will those who receive the abundance of grace and the free gift of righteousness reign in life through the one man Jesus Christ' (v. 17). Here as in 1 Cor. 15 it is Christ who is the central figure and Adam who is the foil, and being in Adam does not completely explain being in Christ.

Can we get help by examining the use of Adam in Jewish tradition? In the Genesis story, *Adam* is the Hebrew word for a human being. At least in some later Jewish circles, this equivalence of Adam with humanity was taken very seriously. An often quoted saying from the Syriac Apocalypse of Baruch (*2 Apoc. Bar.* 54: 19) is: 'Adam is therefore not the cause, save only of his own soul but each of us has become the Adam of his own soul.' Not all later Jewish circles were especially interested in Adam, however, and certainly not all regarded him as responsible for human sin or even as its representative instance. One strand of thought put the blame for the introduction of sin into the world on the ravishing of human women by the angelic powers (Gen. 6) and not on Adam at all. Generally there was less emphasis on Adam's sin than on his glorious perfections which will be restored at the End. Here he quite obviously means Mankind; his individuality is almost totally eclipsed. Sometimes he is described as of gigantic size, presumably because he stands for all humanity.

At all events, for a couple of centuries either side of Paul, there was a concentration of Jewish thought on Adam in some circles, which focused on his perfections before the Fall and the restoration of those perfections in the age to come. He was not merely the first man, but Man, a representative figure. The hope for a renewed Adam was a hope for a renewed humanity.

Paul appears to differ from this tradition in two important ways. First, unlike it on the whole, he emphasizes the sin and not the original perfection of Adam. Secondly, again unlike it so far as we know, he conceives of humanity as being *in* Adam. Both these differences probably arise from the fact that his primary interest is in the last not the first Adam. It is because we can be in Christ that we can be thought of as in Adam, not vice versa. Our examination of two Adam-Christ passages has therefore helped us only to a limited extent. It has helped in that we know that Paul is talking about humanity in its two possible manifestations. We also know that being in Christ means life and righteousness. The help is limited, however, because we are little nearer to understanding the preposition 'in'. We ought to add that a strong case can be made for finding the Adam-Christ contrast in some other passages, like Rom. 1: 18–25; 7: 7–11, 14–25; and as we have seen, Phil. 2: 6–11. In none of these, unfortunately, is the corporate language which concerns us explicitly present.

Corporate language: 3. The body of Christ

Paul uses 'body' (Greek *sōma*) for the community of believers, the church. In the later letters, Colossians and Ephesians, the idea is significantly developed, but for the present we shall consider only the undisputed epistles. We shall also confine ourselves as much as possible to *sōma* as applied to the church, without getting too involved in the debate about its anthropological meaning.

The idea occurs in slightly differing forms in three main passages. We start with Rom. 12: 4f: 'For as in one body we have many members, and all the members do not have the same function, so we, though many, are one body in Christ, and individually members one of another.' There follows an enumeration of differing gifts within the community and then an appeal for love (vv. 6–10). Paul does not here say that the church is the body of Christ, but that it is one body in Christ. On its own, therefore, this passage says little more than the 'in Christ' language generally, which we have already seen to be largely corporate. Moreover, we have here basically a comparison between the body and the church, arguably not going beyond simile. The church is like a body with its various members, in Christ.

The second passage — which preceded Rom. 12 chronologically — is 1 Cor. 12: 12–30: 'For just as the body is one and has many members, and all the members of the body, though many, are one body, so it is with Christ. For by one Spirit we were all baptized into one body — Jews or Greeks, slaves or free — and all were made to drink of one Spirit' (vv. 12f). There follows a detailed enumeration of the body's parts in their variety and mutual dependence, vv. 14–26, and then in vv. 28–30 a demonstration of the mutually dependent and various gifts within the church, linked by the statement in v. 27 that '. . . you are the body of Christ and individually members of it'. Whether Paul takes the church's unity for granted and defends its diversity, or assumes its diversity and argues for its unity, the total picture is clearly one of unity in diversity.

The third passage comes a little earlier in the same letter, when Paul states the incompatibility of taking part both in the Christian eucharist and in pagan cultic celebrations, 1 Cor. 10: 16f: 'The cup of blessing which we bless, is it not a participation in the blood of Christ? The bread which we break, is it not a participation in the body of Christ? Because there is one loaf, we who are many are one body, for we all partake of the same loaf.' Although this passage mainly concerns the exclusive nature of belonging to Christ, it also contains the idea that Christians as a corporate unity share in Christ's body (and blood). It is not just that, as in Rom. 6, believers share in the death and resurrection of Christ. There is the implication that they are his body.

In all these passages Paul sees Christians forming a corporate entity, which in itself is understandable enough, but there is something more. In Rom. 12 believers are one body in Christ. In 1 Cor. 10 they are one body because they share in one loaf; this does not strictly follow: are they one blood because they share in one cup? The notion of being one body must have been in the background already in order to explain the logical leap. Most striking of all, in 1 Cor. 12 where we expect Paul to say (v. 12) 'so it is with the church', he rather says 'so it is with Christ'. Christ himself emerges as the corporate entity analogous to the human body. Once again we meet plainly corporate language about the risen and glorified Christ.

There is much discussion about what Paul means by *sōma*, in particular whether he normally means simply the physical body, or the person as a whole, or perhaps the whole person represented by the physical. For our present question all are equally difficult. It is as hard to understand how a collection of people can equal the whole person of Christ as to see how they can equal his physical body. Even if we say that while for us the body is primarily that which marks out our individuality, our separateness, for Paul it primarily represents the means of relationship with one another, the difficulty is still that he says believers *are* Christ's body. To be one in Christ (Gal. 3: 28) and to be one body in Christ (Rom. 12: 5) may well be the same, but this does not solve the problem either.

How far it was an innovation to equate a group of people with a body is disputed. It is possible that it was new with Paul, but certainly he was not the first to see a group as *like* a body, bound together in mutual dependence. The comparison had been known from the time of Livy (ii. 32) who tells of its use by Menenius Agrippa to talk the plebs out of revolution. It is well attested among the Stoics and the Gnostics. In fact it is a rather obvious figure to use and we need not suppose any particular source for Paul's use of it, though he may have been the one to initiate the move from comparison to equation, not a great step anyway. What is more problematic is his equation of a community with a person, Christ, and with the body of a named historical individual. How can this be?

Among many answers, four are most highly favoured. The first is that, especially in Stoic thought, the commonwealth of mankind was a body, the whole integrally related and mutually necessary in its parts. The organized state was particularly in mind. This usage may well have facilitated Paul's, but it does not altogether explain it, for it does not account for the community's being the body of a named individual. There is no evidence that Paul first thought of the church as a body, in Stoic fashion, and then added to the original idea the complicating 'of Christ' or 'in Christ'.

A second suggestion is that 1 Cor. 10: 16f is the key, and that it was eucharistic practice that led to the identification of the community with Christ's body. Sharing in one loaf, perhaps originally to demonstrate solidarity with the community of the lifetime of Jesus and sharing in his death and resurrection, may have given rise to the idea. Eucharistic practice may indeed have reinforced such an identification, but the logical gap between sharing in something and being that something, as we have already observed, leads us to suspect that the idea was already in existence.

The third suggestion is that although there is no precise analogy between Paul's language and earlier or contemporary ideas, the nearest we can get is Rabbinic talk about the body of Adam. We cannot confidently date this back to Paul's time, but soon afterwards we do meet the idea of the gigantic body of Adam which contained all the souls that would be born. The parallel is hardly exact, for once born the souls were no longer in Adam, but there are obvious advantages to this explanation. It links up with the Adam–Christ contrast of Rom. 5 and 1 Cor. 15; it ties in one corporate usage with another; and it provides a named individual's body in whom the unity exists. However, the last advantage also proves a weakness, for in this Rabbinic talk Adam the individual is almost totally submerged beneath Adam as humanity. In other words it is unlikely that in the body of Adam language we really do have the inclusion of a group of individuals within another individual.

The fourth suggestion finds the key in Gnosticism, but as this leads us beyond the body of Christ to the whole corporate idea, we shall deal with it in the next section. It is time, in fact, that we looked at the corporate language as a whole to see what sense can be made of it. Special explanations have failed in the case of 'the body of Christ', but perhaps there is some way of explaining corporate language in all three manifestations.

The meaning of corporate language about Christ

It is possible that what is totally incomprehensible to us was fully comprehensible to people of Paul's time. On the assumption that Paul really does see Christ as an individual who incorporates other individuals within himself, several explanations have been offered, though there is one which denies the assumption. Thus Rudolf Bultmann in his famous *Theology of the New Testament* (vol. I) argues that some of the language (the 'body of Christ') is explicable in Gnostic terms, and that 'in Christ' is simply a way of talking about the church. All that Paul is really concerned about is the new self-understanding of the individual brought about by the gospel. Yet the amount of evidence seems too great to be disposed of in this way. In particular, most difficult to explain away are those passages where the corporate language is scarcely present on the surface yet is required to make sense of what is said.

Of explanations which assume some sort of 'corporate Christ', two are most notable. The first is the Gnostic one, that Paul either consciously or unconsciously exploits the idea that the Redeemer is incomplete without the redeemed, that the fragments of divinity imprisoned within human beings since a pre-cosmic fall are needed for the original wholeness to be restored. When the elect know their true nature and turn to the Redeemer, they enter him and in a quite literal sense are *in* him, or at least will be when restoration is complete. Sometimes they are specifically in his *body*. Why can all this not be what Paul has in mind?

First, because if Paul believed this he would have no quarrel with Gnostics but would be one of them. Yet in some of his writings (e.g. 1 Corinthians, and Colossians too if he wrote it) he appears to argue against an incipient Gnosticism. Secondly, when he discusses the believer's relationship with Christ in heaven, he talks not of being in Christ but of being *with* Christ, who thus remains a person distinct from his people, however closely related to them (see Phil. 1: 23). In 1 Cor. 15, which is preoccupied with the future of Christians, the only time he comes anywhere near saying that after the resurrection they will be in Christ is v. 22: '. . . so also in Christ shall all be made alive'. This, however, concerns how the resurrection happens, not the resulting condition. In v. 49 he says not that believers will be in Christ, but that they will bear his image (see also 2 Cor. 5: 1–10). Thirdly, as we have seen, it is extremely doubtful whether the Redeemer myth existed until a couple of centuries after Paul.

The second notable explanation of 'corporate Christ' language is the Hebrew notion of corporate personality. This, it is supposed, could conceive of an individual (like the patriarchs, or the Messiah) who also included other people within himself, and rested on a very strong view of the solidarity of the people of Israel. Up to a point we can understand this, even from our individualistic culture, for we know what it is to identify ourselves with a family, a city, a team, or a country. Did we win? is a meaningful question even though 'we' had nothing to do with the victory. We even know what it is to have a representative for our solidarity, like Uncle Sam and John Bull. What we do not have is any notion that such representative figures actually exist, and incorporate — without any loss of identity on either side — those whom they represent. Again, we can have very close relationships with others, but cannot be *in* them, especially without losing individuality. Yet what is impossible for us may have been perfectly possible for people of another age and another culture. It is suggested that Israel did find corporate personality a meaningful idea and that Paul takes it for granted.

No one is likely to deny that Hebrew thinking was more corporate and more concerned with solidarity than ours. Reference is often made to the story of Achan in Josh. 7, where one man's sin was expunged by killing not only the offender but also his family and his animals. The belief that no man is an island was taken with the utmost seriousness. All that Achan possessed was regarded as infected and was destroyed, even his tent. Perhaps more to the point, it is held that certain key figures like patriarchs, kings, and the 'Suffering Servant' of Isa. 40–55, were regarded as not only representative but inclusive of the nation of Israel. One of the more obvious indications of the idea is that Israel (Jacob) was both an individual and the whole nation.

Yet, without any dispute about the importance of solidarity, 'corporate personality' as a Hebrew notion is now under grave question. The Achan case may be a matter of ritual or moral pollution rather than anything more abstruse. More important, while the Old Testament and later Judaism easily conceived of representative figures, it is not clear that they ever envisaged corporate figures, whether kings, patriarchs, Adam, or anyone else. We saw that Adam could be Everyman, but found no good reason to suppose that as an individual he could include other individuals. It is now very doubtful whether there ever was a Hebrew idea of corporate personality which could explain Paul's language.

It thus does not seem that there was a key either in Gnosticism or in Hebrew corporate thinking which can unlock Paul's ideas for us. It is not that Paul's first readers had some habit of mind alien to us, or not demonstrably so. Nevertheless, if we look again at his way of talking about Christ as more than an individual, there are several clues which make it not as difficult to comprehend as at first appears.

The first clue is the equivalence of being in Christ and being in the Spirit, which emerges from passages like Rom. 8 and 1 Cor. 15: 45b, and which we discussed on pp. 46–8. The exalted Christ is now Spirit, and we noted that in the Old Testament the Spirit is always power. In Paul too the Spirit is power, divine power, which liberates from other powers such as Law, sin, and death, and which produces the ethical fruits and the gifts of service that mark the new life of the Christian community (see 1 Thess. 1: 5; 1 Cor. 2: 4; 12: 4–11; 2 Cor. 3: 6; Gal. 5: 18, 22f, 25; Rom. 8: 2; 15: 13). To be in Christ now is to be in the Spirit, i.e. within the sphere of his power. That is to say, the equivalence of the two expressions indicates that Christ as exalted is now a centre of power, so that to be in him means, not to be in his person, but to be in his sphere of power. Moreover, because Christ brings the New Age and because the Spirit is a characteristic of that age, to be in Christ is to be in the power of God's new regime. Life in Christ is therefore the opposite of life under the old dominations and powers (see the next chapter).

Here in fact is our second clue, for these other dominations can be represented in parallel expressions. We can be 'under the law' (Rom. 3: 19a, RSV), but the Greek preposition is not 'under' but 'in'. We can also be in or under sin, where sin is an enslaving power: Rom. 3: 9; 5: 21; 6: 1, 6, 12–14, 17f, 20, 22; 7: 14, 17, 20, 25; 8: 2; 1 Cor. 15: 56f; Gal. 3: 22. One power can be countered only by another, and if we are to avoid being in (under) sin, we must be in (under) Christ, see also 1 Cor. 9: 21. It is relevant that in one Synoptic passage, Mark 3: 22/Luke 11: 15/

Matt. 12: 24 (also Matt 9: 34), where Jesus is accused of working miracles by the power of Beelzebul, the preposition 'in' is what is rendered by 'by the power of'. The point made in the story is that Jesus is accused of working 'in' (by the power of) Beelzebul. Here too to be in something or someone is to be under a power.

The third clue pointing in the same direction is that although in many 'in Christ' contexts there is no clear indication of meaning, where there is the stress frequently falls on belonging to Christ in the sense of being within his sphere of power and influence. So, in 1 Cor. 1: 30 the whole of life is in Christ Jesus, wisdom, righteousness, sanctification, and redemption, and behind him is God as final source (see also 2 Cor. 1: 21). Life in his sphere is freedom from all other powers (Gal. 2: 4; 3: 24–6; 5: 6). This power is the same as that manifested in the resurrection of Christ which will finally effect the resurrection of believers in him (Phil. 3: 9–11). Also pointing in this direction is the expression 'boasting in Christ' (Rom. 15: 17; 1 Cor. 15: 31; Phil. 1: 25f); this makes sense if we take Paul to mean that all his achievements, which are real, are none the less solely the result of his being in Christ, are done in his power and under his lordship, and thus reflect Christ's working in and through him. Of course there is also a sense in which being in Christ is weakness not strength (see especially 2 Cor. 13: 4; Phil. 4: 13); those who are in him acknowledge that they have no strength at all, and Paul's own weakness and insignificance is an important part of his message to the Corinthians. Underlying this is the belief that the person who is in Christ is stamped not only by the power of the resurrection, as in Phil. 3: 9–11, but also by the humiliation of the cross, as in Phil. 3: 10 (cf. 2 Cor. 13: 4).

If we are right about these clues, being in Christ is not as unintelligible as at first appears. It means that Christ is now seen as a centre of divine power, the power of the Spirit, and this confirms our earlier conclusion that seeing him as now Spirit is a significant step forward in Christology. He is still an individual, and there is no confusion of identity between him and those who are in him, but because he is a power-centre he can no longer be thought of in isolation from his people. The corporate language may mean more than this; there may be aspects of it that escape us, but it means at least this. In the end, therefore, it means that believers corporately live under his power and authority.

This interpretation includes our second and third instances of corporate language, the two Adams and the body of Christ. Just as Christ represents the power of the New Age, so Adam represents the power of sin and death. This is especially clear in Rom. 5: 12–21, but it also underlies 1 Cor. 15: 21–3, 45ff. Adam stands for limited humanity, humanity in bondage, but Christ stands for humanity under grace and the divine power, free humanity. As for the body of Christ, it is in no way equivalent to Christ as a person, but is the community of those who live by and under the divine power. This is particularly evident in Rom. 12: 4f, 'one body in Christ', but also in 1 Cor. 12: 12–31 where the apparent equation of the church with Christ in v. 12 must be understood in the light of the whole argument, which is that the church is the body empowered and controlled and defined by the Spirit (see especially vv. 13 and 1–11). 'So also is Christ' in v. 12 is thus a condensed expression for this view, which is more fully set out in v. 27, 'Now you are the body of Christ and individually members of it', and which rests on the understanding of the church as the community of the Spirit.

The notion of being 'members of Christ' found in 1 Cor. 12 cannot be taken just as it stands. It means that Christians belong to and are parts of the corporate entity that derives its existence from Christ through the Spirit. It does not mean that they make up Christ in the way that members of a football club make up that club. Otherwise the identity either of Christ or of the members would be lost, and such a loss of identity is never contemplated by Paul.

The gospel itself is power (Rom. 1: 16) which enables anyone who hears it and responds to it to be transferred from old powers and dominions, represented by Adam, sin, death, and so on, to this new and liberating power. How this transfer occurs will be the subject of the next chapter, but meanwhile we need to note that on the human side it is fundamentally by faith. Indeed, having faith in Christ and being 'found in him' are in the end the same thing (see Phil. 3: 9; Gal. 3: 25–9).

Israel and the church

According to Paul, the church as the community of the last Adam, the community in Christ, is now God's people to be entered by faith. If entry is by faith, it cannot be by anything else, such as belonging racially to the people of israel or adherence to the Law (see especially Gal. 3). Moreover, if Christ is the divinely appointed centre of God's people, there cannot be a competing centre. Yet Paul as a Jew cannot ignore the fact that God already has a people, historical Israel. It was not just a matter of theology, for by its very existence down the street or around the corner the synagogue raised the issue of where the Christians belonged: within the synagogue, within the synagogue and the Christian community as separate entities, or only within the Christian community? No doubt the problem was most acute for Jewish Christians, but it existed almost as sharply for those Gentile Christians who had been (were?) adherents of the synagogue, and could not easily be overlooked even by Christians with no personal history of attachment to the Jewish community. The question was inescapable: what is the relation between the old people and the new? A simple answer could have been, None. As Christ the last Adam brings in the New Age, all that belongs to the old is at best fulfilled and at worst superseded.

Paul comes closest to this negative view in Galatians where he seems to say that the Law has had its day, that the covenant on Mount Sinai is superseded, and indeed that both Law and covenant were diversions from the better and prior covenant with Abraham which was purely a matter of faith and promise (Gal. 4: 21–31 and 3: 6–9, 15–18). This covenant always had the Gentiles in mind and is now fulfilled in Christ and his people. The period between Abraham and Christ (his true seed) is a parenthesis and the true people of God live around that parenthesis. Nevertheless he cannot bring himself to ignore those who claim descent from Abraham and live by the Law, so he regards them as kept in bondage until, together with Gentile Christians, they can enter the heritage of the promise to Abraham (Gal. 3: 23–9). This is the picture in Gal. 3.

The allegory of Gal. 4 seems to give a slightly different picture. Here the Mount Sinai covenant together with the Law and Judaism as it stands represent a covenant of bondage and come from the Hagar-Ishmael line. They are less a temporary stage than a totally wrong direction, for the Sarah-Isaac line has nothing to do with the Mount Sinai covenant or (presumably) the Law. Though this is not quite the same account as in Gal. 3, its effect is similar: the historical people of Israel has become unimportant. It is Abraham (through Isaac) and his seed (Christ and his people) who constitute the people of God. Being a Jew or a Gentile, being circumcised or uncircumcised, keeping the Law or not, are not what matters (Gal. 3: 28f; 6: 15), unless someone starts insisting on them, when they become positive stumbling-blocks. That is, the covenant and Law under which Israel lived are either later intrusions for a temporary purpose and in any case not directly from God (Gal. 3: 17–19), or else a false alternative to the true covenant of freedom (Gal. 4: 21–31).

That seems to be that, except for two things. First, even in Galatians Paul often quotes the Old Testament, whose use constitutes a theological time-bomb bound to explode into the problem of God's promises to Israel. Secondly, he cannot escape the concrete existence of a people who for centuries have lived by what they believe to be God's Law and covenant and who believe that they are the children of Abraham. Neither of these problems is faced in Galatians, but both will have to be defused in due course.

It is in Romans that we meet Paul's more careful reflection on the relationship between the two communities, both claiming to be the people of God. In Galatians he is resisting an attack by Judaisers of some kind, whether Jewish Christians who want all Christians to keep the basics of the Law, or Gentile Christians who have discovered the Jewish roots of their faith and want to embrace at least some aspects of Judaism. In resisting their attack, Paul can give no quarter to Judaism (1 Thess. 2: 13–16 may be even more negative: because of their attacks on Christians, the Jews are under divine condemnation. However, this passage concerns not Israel as such but those members of it who were persecutors). In 2 Cor. 3: 4–18 the extreme position of Galatians is moderated, and in this admittedly difficult passage we seem to have the idea that the Mount Sinai covenant is not abrogated, but confirmed by means of a new interpretation in the light of Christ. The essence of this new interpreation is that — rightly understood — the covenant includes both Jews and Gentiles. Christ removes the veil which obscures true understanding of the giving of the covenant.

This positive approach of 2 Cor. 3 forms a bridge between Galatians and the more mature account in Romans. Perhaps, as some interpreters argue, Paul is setting down his theological position in an atmosphere free from polemics. Perhaps, as others argue, he is trying to reconcile Gentile and Jewish Christian groups within the Roman church. Whatever the reason, Romans faces the question less controversially and less negatively, within the whole perspective of God's dealings with the human race. There is now no doubt that Israel is (not was) God's people, Rom. 9: 4f: 'They are Israelites, and to them belong the sonship, the glory, the covenants, the giving of the law, the worship, and the promises; to them belong the patriarchs, and of their race, according to the flesh, is the Christ.'

The centrality of Christ is in no way modified in Romans, yet Paul does not now discard historical Israel as unimportant and he finds a more positive place for her than he did in Galatians. He has two basic and interrelated problems: first, the relation of the new people of God to the old, and second, how can it be that God's people rejected his Messiah and is now consequently, so it seems, rejected by God? Rom. 9–11 deals almost entirely with these problems, though in Rom. 4 he has already claimed, as in Galatians, that it is those who share Abraham's faith and no others who are his true heirs. There is much in Rom. 9–11 whose meaning is obscure, but his answer to the questions appears to be somewhat as follows.

1. God did indeed elect Israel as his people, but this was never meant to be a simple racial matter. Not all physical descendants of Abraham ever were his true theological descendants, but only those who responded to and lived in the

promise to Abraham (9: 6–8; cf. 4: 9–12). Moreover, God is sovereign, and there has always been selection within the election. Even now there is a remnant within historical Israel which has responded to Christ's fulfilment of the promise and thus maintains the continuity (9: 6–13, 27; 11: 1–5).

2. While the majority have missed this fulfilment (11: 7), yet God's long-term strategy includes the rejection of Christ by the mass of Israel, the mission to the Gentiles and the entry of large numbers of them into his people, and finally an awakening of Israel as a whole to what has happened and their eventual ingathering (11: 11f, 25–32). At present, therefore, they are not true Israel, nor exactly non-Israel. They have tendered their resignation as Israel, all unwittingly. This resignation lies on the table and will not finally be accepted.

3. Meanwhile the relation of the Gentile Christians to God's ancient people is like an olive tree which has had some of its unfruitful branches lopped off in pruning and which has had branches from another tree grafted in instead. This other tree is the wild olive which produces no edible fruit but whose branches, when grafted into the cultivated olive, can become fruitful. The ingrafting and pruning do not preclude the hope that the lopped off branches may eventually be grafted back in again. This analogy (11: 17–24) shows how Paul wishes to maintain the continuity of the church with Israel and how, far from turning his back on Israel, he sees the Christian community as the true heir of the past, the people of God as God wants it to be.

It is not surprising that, except possibly in Gal. 6: 16, Paul does not simply refer to the church as Israel, for the reality is more complicated. Israel, beginning with Abraham, includes all those faithful to the promise, all who have faith and rely only on God, and now above all those who respond to Christ the true seed. This is why in becoming a Christian Paul did not think he was converted from Judaism — he never left it — but was rather converted to being a true Israelite and a true child of Abraham (it was probably not until after the Jewish war of 66–70 that Christians began to see themselves as outside Israel).

Paul's dilemma, never fully resolved, is that there is only one people of God, as old as Abraham and as new as Jesus Christ, yet that in Christ there is neither Jew nor Greek, so that Judaism as it now is, embracing circumcision, the Law, and being of the historical Israel, is irrelevant (see Galatians, but also Phil. 3: 4–7). Yet somehow he cannot bring himself to write historical Israel off: in Rom. 11, as we saw, he expresses the hope that at the End all Israel will be gathered in without saying that they will become Christian.

As a postscript, we may observe that his doctrine of election in Rom. 9–11 primarily concerns peoples not individuals. He is talking about God's choice of a people to serve him in the world, not about whether this person or that gets to heaven. No doubt it is possible to draw conclusions about the fate of individuals, and certainly Rom. 8: 28–30 can be read in an individualist way, but his primary concern is who is the people of God. Undoubtedly he envisages divine choice and therefore divine rejection, but much that is sometimes said about the predestination of individuals to salvation or damnation is later interpretation and not what Paul himself is talking about.

A people of the future living in the present world

The people of Christ, the last Adam, is the people of the End and the New Age, the people of the future as well as the seed of Abraham. It is also the people of the Spirit, who is a sign of the End. Indeed Paul calls the Spirit an *arrabōn* (2 Cor. 1: 22; 5: 5; cf. Eph. 1: 14) which has its closest modern parallel in hire purchase and the deposit system. A deposit has two functions; it is both the promise of the full payment to be made in due course, and the first instalment of that payment. Similarly the Spirit as an *arrabōn* (RSV 'guarantee') is both the promise of the future inheritance and its first instalment. The same idea is conveyed when the Spirit is called the 'first fruits', the image coming from the harvest (Rom. 8: 23). To live in the Spirit is thus partly to live in present enjoyment of a future inheritance and also to have the assurance of its coming fullness. The church is then the community of the future.

This is also seen in 1 Cor. 15 where the argument is that Christians will be raised with Christ, see especially vv. 20-3. Because they are in the last Adam who was raised, they know they too will be raised. Their roots may lie in the past with Abraham, but because they now live in Christ the focus of their life is in the future. Meanwhile, in so far as they represent that future they are an anomaly, for they have embraced the End that is signalled by Christ's death and resurrection, but that will not be consummated until his glorious return.

Yet this future people lives wihin the present doomed world, and therefore needs its own structures and ministries. In the undisputed Pauline letters these are rudimentary and loose. So far as we know, Christians always met in private houses, which must have put a limit on the size of a congregation (see Rom. 16, especially vv. 5, 14f; 1 Cor. 16: 19; Philem. 2). If the Corinthian church was typical, worship was unplanned and even sometimes chaotic (1 Cor. 14; 26-40) as all who claimed inspiration tried to have their say.

Ministries too, at least in Corinth, were charismatic, reflecting the gifts the Spirit bestowed on individuals (1 Cor. 12: 8-11, 28-30). Of elders we hear not at all and of bishops and deacons only in Phil. 1: 1. The ministry in which Paul shows most interest is his own apostolic one, and that of associates like Timothy, Barnabas, Titus, and Silvanus (1 Thess. 1: 1; Gal. 2: 1, 3; 1 Cor. 4: 17; 9: 6; 2 Cor. 1: 19; Rom. 16: 21). The overall picture shows little structure or organized authority. Even Paul as an apostle, though he claims divine authority and can on occasion simply issue a command (as in 1 Cor. 5: 3), more often argues his case.

Things could not stay like this, and we shall see that in the next generation Pauline churches were quite tightly organized, but meanwhile life was in the power of the Spirit under the lordship of Christ. Even in Phil. 1: 1 we are not sure whether bishops and deacons are offices, or merely functions of oversight (bishops) and practical service (deacons) which may have been exercised by the same people. In general, Paul is more interested in the church's place in God's pattern of salvation than in its organization.

His main interest in baptism is its expression of dying and rising with Christ (Rom. 6) and of belonging to Christ as Lord (1 Cor. 1: 12–17). In his brief discussions of the eucharist in 1 Cor. 10: 16–21 and 11: 20–33 he sees it as looking back to the death of Jesus, as conveying a present fellowship of participants with one another and their lord, and as pointing forward to the messianic banquet. In other words it reflects his general view of the church as living on the edge of the times. It seems not to have been rigidly structured, for in 1 Cor. 11: 20–33 Paul is anxious about the fact that, as in many contemporary banquets, much better food was being served to the rich than to the poor.

Conclusion

In all this we see how central for Paul was the person of Jesus Christ. To talk about the church was to talk about him, its Lord and the centre of power in which it lived. Christ is the definitive act and revelation of God, and is already moving beyond straightforward humanness. Moreover, to talk about him was also to talk about his people, not just as individuals but as a corporate whole, for he cannot be seen as an isolated figure. It is Christ and his people, together, that are in view.

5

Old Life and New

If for Paul Christ represents the shift of the ages and makes a new beginning for the human race, how does he see the two alternative possibilities of life, and how do people move from one to the other?

Salvation

According to Rom. 1: 16 the gospel is 'the power of salvation to every one who has faith'. If we ask what salvation is, the answer is not always clear nor always the same, but is generally to do with life and freedom: life, because the goal is life under God now and in the future; freedom, because powers which oppress and harm humanity are now overcome. People can live with and for God, free from the penalties which follow life in opposition to him (e.g. 1 Thess. 5: 8–10; Rom. 5: 9). Most of the instances of 'save' words, however, have no specific reference, but as hopes for salvation were common enough at the time, Paul probably had no need to spell out what he meant.

In the Hellenistic world people wanted salvation (liberation) from what inhibited their full enjoyment of life, most notably the fear of death and the sense of helplessness before fate. They feared not total annihilation, but mere shadowy, attenuated existence after death, and they longed for something that would be an accentuation not a diminution of present life, at least of its agreeable features. Further, whether or not they believed in the stars' control of human destiny, they feared that freedom of choice was an illusion. The Jews on the other hand were traditionally more concerned about national freedom and their future as a people, and longed for liberation from foreign, anti-Yahweh, domination, and for that wholeness of corporate life which would follow liberation and would include justice, prosperity, and well-being. Long before Paul's time many had come to believe that it could be realized only in a totally new order, in the Age to Come.

Paul believed that with Christ the End had begun. Of course, its fullness must await the return of Christ in glory to establish God's reign (see especially 1 Thess. 4: 13–17; 1 Cor. 15: 22–8). Yet whether that consummation is imminent or not, Christians are the people of the End-time, and their salvation which belongs to the future is already present in some measure. In good Jewish fashion Paul often speaks of salvation as future, e.g. Rom. 13: 11: 'Salvation is nearer to us now than when we first believed.' See also the 'hope of salvation' in 1 Thess. 5: 8, and the future tense of the verb 'save' in 1 Cor. 3: 15; 5: 5; Rom. 5: 9f; 9: 27; 10: 9. This is what we should expect. The new life, stronger than death, belongs to the New Age and awaits its arrival. Yet because the End has begun, salvation is becoming a present reality, and Christians are those who are in the process of being saved: 'For the word of the cross is folly to those who are perishing, but to us who are being saved it is the power of God' (1 Cor, 1: 18; cf. also 15: 2; 2 Cor. 2: 15; 6: 2).

In the lives of those who belong to Christ, the End's realities are anticipated. This is evident in the one place where Paul goes so far as to use 'save' in the past tense, but where he also at once qualifies this with a future reference: '. . . we ourselves, who have the first fruits of the Spirit, groan inwardly as we wait for adoption as sons, the redemption of our bodies. For in this hope we were saved' (Rom. 8: 23b–4). The New English Bible is more illuminating when it renders the last sentence 'For we have been saved, though only in hope.' The tension between the 'already' and the 'not yet' is thus admirably stated. What belongs to the future has already begun, in advance. But what is thus enjoyed, and what are the things from which believers in Christ are freed?

Liberated from sin

Paul nowhere delineates his doctrine of sin, but it is clear enough that he sees it under two aspects: it is both what we do by choice, voluntary action, and also a power whose grip we cannot escape simply by deciding to. It is thus both our responsibility, and something we cannot help!

On the voluntary and culpable side, it is a turning away from God to something less than God, treating as ultimate what is not ultimate. In Rom. 1: 18–32, especially vv. 21, 25, 28, Paul indicts the human race of knowing enough of God to live by, of knowing the difference between the Creator's deity and the world's created character, yet of deliberately turning from Creator to creature and of seeking security there. In the Gentile world, this in practice meant idolatry, worshipping things that are part of creation. Nobody in the world has any excuse for this, because

> Ever since the creation of the world his invisible nature, namely, his eternal power, and deity, has been clearly perceived in the things that have been made. So they are without excuse; for although they knew God they did not honour him as God or give thanks to him, but they became futile in their thinking and their senseless minds were darkened. Claiming to be wise they became fools, and exchanged the glory of the immortal God for images resembling mortal man or birds or reptiles. (Rom. 1: 20–3)

So far no Jew would disagree. Whether or not in the form of idolatry, it is culpable to treat as God, what is not God. Notice, however, the strong hint about the consequent loss of freedom: 'their senseless minds were darkened', they became incapable of anything better. This hint is reinforced in the rest of the chapter where every kind of wickedness and perversion, but especially sexual kinds, arise from this fundamental turning from God to not-God. We shall see later in this chapter that sin's propensity to multiply itself, to increase in a downward spiral of self-propelling wickedness, is seen by Paul as a manifestation of the wrath of God. Accelerating decadence and degradation are the marks of lives that turn from Creator to creature. The list of vices is not meant to be exhaustive, but like ethical lists in the ancient world generally (see Chapter 6), to indicate wholesale wickedness of all sorts against God and against other people. All comes from the basic error.

We have already seen in vv. 20–3 a move from the voluntary to the involuntary. We begin by making culpable wrong choices, but end by not knowing good from bad, or by being unable to escape from the bad when we know it. This is the meaning of 'God gave them up . . .' (vv. 24, 26, 28). God did not restrain them, but allowed them to enmesh themselves in the toils of their own chosen courses. We thus meet the duality in Paul's idea of sin with which we began: it is both a state (Paul is little interested in concrete acts of sin, but more in the alienation from God which produces them), and a force. In the early chapters of Romans the question of sin is dealt with at length, and in 3: 10 there is a peroration in which all people, Jews and Gentiles, are found sinful. We also come to the conclusion, 3: 9, that 'all men, both Jews and Greeks, are under the power of sin'. They are not free. This perception may well explain the omission of any emphasis on repentance and forgiveness in Paul's letters, a decisive difference from contemporary Judaism. His diagnosis of the human condition is more pessimistic than that of his contemporaries, who believed that all sinners could repent, be forgiven, and then by following the Torah lead righteous lives if they really wanted to. Paul believes they cannot. All are trapped and controlled by the power of sin whether they like it or not. Repentance and forgiveness are therefore not enough: what is needed is liberation by a superior force. Sin is slavery, although it begins by consent. Perhaps a parallel is alcoholism: the alcoholic begins by choosing to drink, and ends by drinking whether he chooses or not.

Paul may be building on the Jewish belief in an Evil Impulse, which oppresses people and is always at war with the Good Impulse, though the Torah could be fulfilled and was indeed a weapon against the Evil Impulse. Paul did not agree about the Torah, but certainly he can talk about sin as an external enslaving power (Rom. 3: 9; 6: 6, 20; 7: 14; see also 'sin reigned in death' Rom. 5: 21, and the expressions in Rom. 7: 9, 11, 17–20 which, perhaps figuratively, depict sin as an independent agent). We have already seen that in the Adam–Christ passage Rom. 5: 12–21 the way of Adam is the way of bondage. Human beings in Adam need both acquittal and life (v. 18) to deal with the voluntary and the involuntary character of sin.

Even a righteous life under the Law does not ensure freedom from sin, as Paul found in his own experience. It was his zeal for the Law that made him a persecutor of the church (Phil. 3: 6; Gal. 1: 13), something that causes him great distress (1 Cor. 15: 9). This shows that one must go not to the Law but to Christ to know what sin is (Gal. 2: 17f), for anything that dethrones Christ is sin. Moreover, only in Christ, in the power of Christ, is there liberation from this other and sinister power.

Liberated from flesh (*sarx*)

Deliverance from sin is also deliverance from *sarx*. This word, translated 'flesh' in many English versions, has a variety of meanings. Paul can use it as we do to mean the physical stuff of which we are made. In 1 and 2 Corinthians, where he may be arguing against an incipient Gnosticism which depreciated the physical, he can use it quite neutrally (1 Cor. 6: 16; 15: 39; 2 Cor. 7: 1 — translated 'body' in RSV — where he is presumably stressing that the physical is capable of purification, something Gnostics would deny). In other parts of the Corinthian letters (e.g. 1 Cor. 3: 1, 3; 2 Cor. 5: 16), the word has a pejorative meaning like that often found in Galatians and Romans which we shall discuss immediately below. We also find it used in the sense of kinship, as in our expression 'my own flesh and blood' (see Rom. 9: 3 and probably 1 Cor. 10: 18).

What concerns us here is a use which does not occur in 1 Thessalonians and which may have emerged first in the Galatian dispute. It has been plausibly argued that this use, which sees *sarx* as totally and inherently bad but as not exclusively physical, began with the insistence of some people in Galatia that circumcision was necessary to a full Christianity. Perhaps Paul knows that circumcision was sometimes called 'the covenant in the flesh' (Ecclus. 44: 20). Anyway, according to Gal. 3: 3, to move from the sole requirement of faith to the additional requirement of circumcision was to begin with the Spirit and end with 'the flesh' (cf. 6: 13). Behind this contrast there probably lies an opposition between Spirit and flesh, with Spirit representing the New Age, the Age of God, and flesh representing the Old Age, the Age of Belial and wickedness, so that the two terms stand for the two aeons, as in the Qumran Scrolls (see IQS 4, 11). Certainly in the Hagar-Sarah allegory of Gal. 4 flesh and Spirit are two powers, flesh representing life under the Law, and Spirit representing freedom under the gospel. This use may have been facilitated by the Septuagint which regularly uses *sarx* to translate the Hebrew *bāsār* which can sometimes mean human weakness as opposed to divine strength.

Circumcision in Galatians thus stands for relying on something other than Christ alone, which is absurd, for he alone is sufficient. It is also dangerous, for attempting to add to Christ is tantamount to rejecting him, moving from his sole dominion to an alternative one, that of the Law which circumcision represents (Gal. 5: 3). So, *sarx* is used for something physical, circumcision, and is then extended to mean something alternative to Christ. It is not merely an error, but a demonic enslaving power. It is anything other than God in Christ in which we put our final trust. That in Galatians the alternative may be not wrongdoing but the Law does not make it less deadly: to insist on circumcision is to insist on the whole Law, and therefore to be severed from Christ as solely sufficient (Gal. 5: 3f). He will not share his lordship, even with the Law.

Paul is aware that such talk may lay him open to a charge of condoning immorality. In Gal. 5, after stressing that the Christian way is the way of freedom, he warns (v. 13) that this must not be taken as an opportunity for another manifestation of *sarx*, immorality. Christians live not by the Law but by the Spirit, and the Spirit fosters righteousness, not immorality. Life under *sarx* can thus also take the form of libertinism, of doing what pleases us, because in the satisfaction of our desires and in our own self-interest we find the centre and sufficiency of our life. In this chapter, *sarx* and Spirit are again two powers, under only one of which we must live, the power of God (Spirit) which leads to a thoroughly godly and righteous life, and produces fruit like love, joy, peace, patience, and the rest (vv. 22f). Like contemporary ethical lists generally, this one is meant to represent all the good results of living in the Spirit, not just those specified, but it is noteworthy that there is a considerable emphasis on social virtues.

Being in Christ (Gal. 5: 6) and therefore being in the Spirit (Gal. 5: 25) is what believers are. Walking according to the Spirit, that is living out in practice their fundamental belonging, is what they must do (vv. 16, 25). It is not now a matter of charismatic gifts or ministries as in 1 Cor. 12, but of practical good living, in opposition to the life according to the flesh. It is not a matter of physical-centred life as against non-physical-centred life, but of a human centre and rule as against a divine centre and rule. That *sarx* in Gal. 5 is not primarily a matter of physical appetites and indulgence is clear from vv. 19–21: 'Now the works of the flesh are plain: immorality, impurity, licentiousness, idolatry, sorcery, enmity, strife, jealousy, anger, selfishness, dissension, party spirit, envy, drunkenness, carousing, and the like . . .' The list starts with sexual sins, mentions religious sins (idolatry and sorcery), and ends with more sins of the body, sins of excessive indulgence (drunkenness and carousing), but in the middle is a solid block of what can only be called social sins, sins of wrong relationship to others. More than half are in this category, so it is quite clear that life in *sarx* is not simply physical life, but life perverted and misdirected by relying on something other than God. Most of the items on the list have no particular physical reference at all. In short, the *sarx*–Spirit dualism in Paul is not a body–soul dualism, but a 'life under God'–'life under anything else' dualism. To live by the Spirit is to live by God, and to live by the *sarx* is to live by what is not God, whether in itself it is good (like the Law) or bad (like self-gratification). Even the bad things by which one may live can vary greatly from gross physical self-indulgence to envy.

The original connection of this use of *sarx* with the debate about circumcision emerges again in Phil. 3: 3f, but it is in Romans that the terminology comes to fullest expression. In 2 Cor. 10: 2f Paul had drawn a useful distinction between living in the flesh, which is simply bodily life in this present world and therefore ethically neutral, and living according to the flesh, which is submitting to standards and securities other than God. In Romans, however, this distinction is not maintained: in 8: 5–13 to live according to the flesh and to set the mind on the flesh and to be in the flesh are all equivalent. The distance he has moved from seeing *sarx* as merely the physical life in this world is demonstrated by v. 9; 'But you are not in the flesh, you are in the Spirit, if the Spirit of God really dwells in you.' As they obviously are still in the world and still embodied, life in the flesh must mean life not under God. It is not immediately clear in this chapter whether Paul is opposing confidence in the Law or libertinism, but it is certainly anything other than life in Christ (v. 1) and life in the Spirit.

Sarx and sin amount to the same thing (Gal. 5: 19–21; Rom. 7: 5; 8: 3, 10). Like sin, *sarx* is a dominating power and not just a freely chosen option, see Gal. 5: 17; Rom. 7: 5, 18; 8: 12. As such, it needs to be countered by another power, and this is what Gal. 5 is mainly about.

Liberated from Law

Unlike sin, Law is not malignant, and Paul's position on it is so ambivalent that we shall have to consider it at length in Chapter 6. Even in Galatians he never calls it wicked nor denies it a place in the divine purpose (Gal. 3: 23f). It is true that the treatment of Hagar in Gal. 4: 21–31 suggests that the Law's tutelage never was God's will, and to that extent Paul is inconsistent. In Romans, it is fundamentally holy (7: 12), yet in both letters he describes it as something to be liberated from (Gal. 4: 21; 5: 18; Rom. 7: 6). Why? In Galatians one answer is that it was a divinely appointed guardian whose day is now over, so that to remain in its guardianship now that the freedom of Christ and of his Spirit has arrived is anachronistic bondage. Its function was to keep Israel in line, preparing her for the coming freedom (Gal. 3: 21–6). To remain in its tutelage now is to reject the freedom of the sons of God (Gal. 4: 5).

In Romans too the Law is something to be freed from: this is the point of the analogy in Rom. 7: 1–3 with the widow who is now free from her husband's rule. Having died with Christ, believers are now free from the Law that formerly ruled over them, vv. 4–6. He goes further than in Galatians, however, in stating that in itself the Law is good (7: 7, 12, 14), though perverted by *sarx* (8: 3) which exploited the commandment to bring about harm and death (7: 8, 11). Apparently it is the Law's misuse that makes it a hostile power, but he does not here explain what that misuse is, and this too we must examine in Chapter 6.

Liberated from wrath (*orgē*)

'We shall be saved from the wrath' (Rom. 5: 9). The meaning of 'wrath' (*orgē*) has been much disputed, but it certainly does not denote a divine emotion like a loss of temper. C. H. Dodd long ago pointed out a curious reserve in Paul's language: the verb 'to be angry' is never used with God as subject, and though 'the wrath' often occurs, only three times are the words 'of God' added (Rom. 1: 18; Col. 3: 6; Eph. 5: 6, only the first in an undisputed letter). Evidence of this sort led him to conclude that for Paul it is not to do with God's angry attitude, but with cause and effect in a moral universe. If you put your hand in the fire, you suffer pain not because God is angry with you, but because that is how the universe works. Similarly, sin leads to painful consequences not because God in his anger decides to smite you, but because this is a universe of causes and effects, physically and morally.

Now this suggestion fits reasonably well with some 'wrath' passages but not quite all. Though in Jewish literature God's wrath is at work in the current life of the nation (see the persistent theme of the Book of Judges that deserting Yahweh has disastrous consequences), it was believed that it would be particularly evident on the Day of Judgment to vindicate his people against their enemies and oppressors (see for example Isa. 2: 10–22). Dodd's view does not take adequate account of this equation of the Day of Wrath with the Day of Judgment also in Paul (1 Thess. 1: 10; Rom. 2: 5; probably Rom. 5: 9). More probably, the basic idea is that humanity cannot flout God's will without disaster for there will be a reckoning, in the midst of life or at the Judgment. As Dodd saw, it is not that God loses control of his emotions, but that his consistent will opposes evil now and will condemn it at the End. His love is holy love with an inbuilt pressure towards holiness and righteousness. This pressure will be inescapable at the Judgment but is already evident in a preliminary way.

We saw when discussing Rom. 1: 18–32 in connection with sin, that its propensity to accelerate and produce degradation in the lives of those who deliberately turn away from the Creator is an expression of wrath. That passage begins (v. 18): 'For the wrath of God is revealed from heaven against all ungodliness and wickedness of men who by their wickedness suppress the truth.' What follows thus illustrates how wrath works. Similarly, those who possess the Law and have high moral standards, and look critically on the picture of degradation in Rom. 1: 18–32, yet who themselves fail to live up to those standards and obey the Law, also incur *orgē* (Rom. 2: 1–24; 4: 15). Their moral impotence is not healed but exposed by the Law.

On a practical level, the civil power is an agent of God's *orgē* (Rom. 13: 4). The penalties that in any human society follow an infringement of its rules are an expression of wrath: the one in authority 'is God's servant for your good. But if you do wrong, be afraid, for he does not bear the sword in vain; he is the servant of God to execute his wrath on the wrongdoer.' Actions have consequences, and human sanctions are part of the divine pressure towards righteousness. This is closely connected with conscience, probably to be understood as the uncomfortable feelings that afflict those who do something they know is wrong (Rom. 13: 5): 'Therefore one must be subject, not only to avoid God's wrath, but also for the sake of conscience.'

So then, at the last Judgment and during this life, sin has varying consequences which are all reflections of the divine pressure towards righteousness and godliness. Its final penalties are included in the things from which Christ delivers people: 1 Thess. 1: 10; Rom. 5: 9.

Liberated from the powers

Finally, Christ delivers from bondage to the celestial or infernal powers (Rom. 8: 37–9; 1 Cor. 15: 24–7; Gal. 4: 3–7; cf. Col. 2: 14f; Eph. 1: 21f). In Gal. 4: 3–7 and Col. 2: 14f, the Law appears to be classed as such a power, and this may be reflected in the statement in Gal. 3: 19f that it did not come directly from God but indirectly through angels, that is through subordinate powers who may become barriers to God. At all events, Christ has provided deliverance from these powers by his dying and rising. They still exist and still have force, but not over Christians who are now under a superior power. This deliverance is present (Gal. 4 and Col. 2) but also future (Rom. 8 and 1 Cor. 15). The future victory is thus provisionally anticipated in the present for those who share in Christ's victory and so straddle the Ages.

It is clear enough that Paul sees salvation as liberation from other powers to enable life to be henceforth under the power of God. The next question we must take up is how people move from one to the other.

The means of liberation: faith and grace

Rom. 1: 16 tells us that the gospel is power. It is of course power seen above all in weakness, the weakness of Christ on the cross, and is characterized by love not coercion. It is precisely this power that is needed to transfer men and women from the old sinister power-sphere to the new one of freedom and life. It does not do this, however, automatically or in the mass. Humanity is seen corporately, with life under both old and new dominations seen in corporate terms, yet the move from one to the other is also an individual matter. On the human side the transfer happens by faith, and faith involves individuals.

'Faith' (Greek *pistis*, cognate with the verb *pisteuō*, 'believe') has several meanings in Paul, not all of which concern us here.

We are not concerned with faith as a body of beliefs (Gal. 1: 23; 6: 10), nor with it as 'faithfulness' (Rom. 3: 3), but rather with faith as grasping what God offers, as saying 'Yes' to his gracious approach. It is not an action to be performed with effort, indeed it is almost a non-thing. In Rom. 4: 1–6 Paul is at pains to show that it is no kind of work. It is essentially a response to grace, and grace is God's unmotivated goodness. It is unmotivated not because God has no reason for being generous, but because the reason lies within his own nature and not in the merit or attractiveness of the recipient. Grace that is deserved is not grace but reward. So, despite the fact that humanity deserves only opposition from God, God's generosity and goodness lead him to liberate it from what oppresses it and from its own error.

Thus grace (*charis*; see for example Rom. 3: 24; 4: 4, 16; Gal. 2: 21) and faith go hand in hand, the divine offer and the human response. Any attempt to marry faith with some other requirement, such as circumcision, is to be rejected. Faced with God's offer one simply accepts it, and does not try to add something to it. The sufficiency of faith on the human side for salvation is total (see again Rom. 4: 1–8).

It follows from this emphasis on faith, indeed, that any attempt to earn salvation is doomed, but it must be stressed that this is not what Paul appears to be attacking. Rather he opposes any threat to the adequacy of faith in Christ. Naturally it is in contexts dealing with acceptance before God and into his people that the emphasis on faith is most immediately obvious (e.g. Rom. 3: 21 — 4: 25; Gal. 3: 6–26). However the idea that faith is both essential and sufficient occurs much more widely than in the relatively infrequent justification passages.

Faith as response and unconditional commitment to God and his offer of salvation does of course imply beliefs *about* Christ, but this implication is not underlined by Paul. More important is that it involves an element of obedience, but this needs to be stated with caution lest faith be seen as something we do. Perhaps 'commitment' better expresses its ongoing aspect: it is not just that faith effects the move from one domination to another (Rom. 10: 9), or that it is the acceptance of God's free offer

(Rom. 10: 10), but that it is on the human side the condition of continuing life in Christ: 'the life I now live in the flesh I live by faith in the Son of God' (Gal. 2: 20; see also Phil. 3: 9). There are not two faiths, one the initial response and the other the continuing attitude, but only one consistent response and attitude which both enables people to enter Christ's realm and keeps them there (compare Gal. 3: 24 and 26). Because faith is continuing it is possible to think of it as obedience, though not in the sense of an activity. So, Christians participate in the new life of the Spirit through faith (Gal. 3: 1–5), and participate in the death and resurrection of Christ by faith (1 Thess. 4: 14; 2 Cor. 4: 13f; Rom. 6: 8; 10: 9). It is by faith, and not by belonging to the historical people of Israel, that people become true children of Abraham, and enter a new life of freedom and power in Christ and the Spirit.

The means of liberation: reconciliation and redemption

Paul uses several expressions for the means of transfer from one dominion to the other, and in doing so he sometimes has in view human responsiblity for the present state, and sometimes human inability to do anything about it, reflecting his dual view of sin. Reconciliation is more concerned with the first, and redemption with the second.

Humanity needs reconciliation because it is in a state of hostility towards God. Living under and for anything other than God is to be out of true relationship with him, and this must be put right if there is to be peace with him. It is sometimes debated whether the hostility is only on the human side, or whether God too has hostility towards his rebellious subjects and needs to be reconciled. Is reconciliation one-sided or two-sided? It may be said that in any breach of relationship two-sided reconciliation is needed, and that God's hostility to sin is such that his wrath needs to be turned away. Is this how Paul sees it?

If we look at the reconciliation passages (chiefly Rom. 5: 10f and 2 Cor. 5: 18–20, though cf. also Col. 1: 20–2 and Eph. 2: 16), we cannot be sure that he does. It is true that in

Rom. 5: 10f (as in Col. 1: 20, 22 and Eph. 2: 16) Christ's death on the cross makes reconciliation possible, and conceivably what is meant is that God takes that death as payment for sin and so is willing to be reconciled. Nevertheless this is not stated or even hinted at. All we can safely say is that there is a connection between the cross and reconciliation, but that its precise nature is unclear. In 2 Cor. 5: 18–20 there is no doubt that men and women are reconciled to God, not the other way round, despite the fact that the cross is clearly in the background (see vv. 15, 21), and despite our being told in v. 19 that God did not count people's trespasses against them.

The position is less clear in Rom. 5: 10: '. . . while we were enemies we were reconciled to God by the death of his Son . . .' Are the enmity and the reconciliation one- or two-sided? An answer probably cannot come from the passage itself, but from an overall view of what Paul believes about the death of Christ. Even here, however, there is insufficient reason to suppose that God needs to be reconciled. Indeed there is a case for saying that he cannot, if we take seriously what was said about the unmotivated generosity of grace, which always takes the initiative. It is men and women who need to be reconciled to God.

Redemption is a metaphor from the slave market, and responds to the need for liberation from bondage rather than the need for deliverance from guilt and estrangement. Pauline literature uses three words for this: *exagorazō* in Gal. 3: 13 and 4: 5; *lutroō* in Tit. 2: 14; and *apolutrōsis* in Rom. 3: 24; 8: 23; 1 Cor. 1: 30; Col. 1: 14; Eph. 1: 7, 14; 4: 30. All three basically denote transfer from one ownership to another, and in the case of the second and third, transfer from slavery to freedom. In the Septuagint *lutr-* is the root used for Israel's deliverance from slavery in Egypt, so it can scarcely be doubted that 'redemption' in Paul means deliverance from slavery of some sort. There is never, in the Septuagint, any reference to a price, nor is there in Paul, except in 1 Cor. 6: 20 and 7: 23 — 'you were bought with a price' — but here the *lutr-* root is not used. We cannot read into Paul some notion that the death of Christ was the price paid (to the Devil?) to set men and women free, though this is not to deny that redemption is costly. At least occasionally Paul connects it to the cross, Gal. 3: 13; Rom. 3: 24 (and cf. Eph. 1: 7; Tit. 2: 14). What we can be sure about is that he is speaking about change of dominion and about freeing people from what has hitherto held them captive.

If we ask what Christ redeems people from, there are three answers. First, he frees them from the Law and its curse (Gal. 3: 13; 4: 5). Secondly, he frees from sin and its power (Rom. 3: 24; cf. also Col. 1: 14; Eph. 1: 7; Tit. 2: 14). Thirdly he gives them the final freedom of life with God at the End (Rom. 8: 23, perhaps also the non-specific 1 Cor. 1: 30; cf. also Eph. 1: 14; 4: 30). As in the case of reconciliation, the role of the cross cannot be ignored even if it is only sometimes mentioned, and we must shortly examine this role.

The means of liberation: justification

Especially since the Reformation, there has been a strong tradition of interpretation which sees this as the heart of Paul's theology and indeed of Christianity itself. Although it has long been believed that Paul aimed his justification teaching against the idea that men and women could win God's favour by their moral or religious attainment (by 'works'), it now seems very much more likely that his target was different. There may well be hints that he would have shared the Reformers' abhorrence of any idea that we can *achieve* God's good pleasure, e.g. Rom. 4: 2, yet his justification teaching seems rather to have been in opposition to any attempt to impose the Jewish Law, the Torah, on his converts, at least in its entirety. To suggest that Gentile converts need to be circumcised and thereafter live in full obedience to the Torah, is on the one hand to say that Christ and faith in him are not sufficient, and on the other hand, to say that only Jews, or those who are willing to become Jews, can be within God's people (Gal. 2: 11–21; see also 'The means of liberation: faith and grace' above, and 'The Law cannot save', Chapter 6 below). It may be added that to be accepted into the people of God and to be within the favour of God are two sides of one coin; see the letter to the Galatians.

For Paul, then, the only requirement for acceptance with God is faith in Christ. This is 'justification by faith'. Although there has been debate on the point for centuries, it is now usually accepted that the verb 'justify' (the noun 'justification' is rare, found only in Rom. 4: 25 and 5: 18) has to do with the restoration of a relationship and not the establishment of a new character. This is sometimes expressed by saying that it means 'declare righteous' and not 'make righteous' (in Greek 'righteous' and 'justify' are cognate: *dikaios* and *dikaioō*). The difficulty with this way of putting it is that it has God declaring something which is not so, namely that the person in question is righteous. This cannot be rectified by saying that 'righteous' here means 'in a right relationship', for that is not what the word means. The basic trouble is that too much is made of the supposed judicial background of the verb 'justify', as if to justify someone were to acquit him in a court of law. The Septuagintal use of 'justify' (*dikaioō*) for the Hebrew verb *ṣdk* shows that the legal or forensic reference is only one among several, all of which concentrate on the restoration of healthy relationship within the family or tribe or nation, often including the relationship with Yahweh. Moreover, even if a legal background is pressed, the legal system in question was less concerned to pronounce innocent or guilty than to put wrongs right and to restore people to their proper place, no more and no less, in the covenant community. Justification in Paul is thus the act of restoring people to their proper relationship with God. It comes close to forgiveness, with which it is indeed equated in Rom. 4: 6-8.

Some have wanted to see more than this, a positive and qualitative change in the person justified, but when Paul speaks of such a change he rarely if ever uses the language of justification. Justification is strictly acceptance, restoration to fellowship, and not transformation of character (though that will follow). We shall see that justification is part of a whole, and cannot be isolated from other theological ideas which do concern the transformation of character and behaviour, but in itself it does not refer to these things.

Rom. 1: 17 shows that behind God's gracious activity such as in justification, lies the righteousness of God. This is not God's justice in the narrow sense of rewarding the innocent and punishing the guilty, but his faithfulness to his covenant people. In practice more often than not this means his saving activity, now evident in the gospel of Jesus Christ in which God acts to save all who have faith, all who thus become true children of Abraham, whether Jews or Gentiles. It is God's righteousness which makes him justify people who do not deserve it (Rom. 3: 21ff). At the end of this chapter we shall see that Paul also believes that believers are drawn into and share God's righteousness in Christ, and that this makes possible a whole new being.

The derivation of justification from God's righteousness now evident in Christ helps to locate its place in Paul's thought. Albert Schweitzer went too far when he called it a 'subsidiary crater'. It occupies much of Galatians and Romans, and appears also in Phil. 3 and 1 Cor. 6: 11, and in any case the question of people's relationship with God can hardly be a subsidiary one. Nevertheless it is the person of Christ that is central, and it would be a distortion to think of justification by faith simply as a new procedure for acceptance, capable of being maintained separately from Christ. Justification occurs only in and through him and in the end is a way of talking about him. Yet was it originally, and is it essentially, a matter of relationship with God, or was it in the first place worked out to deal with community relationships?

A powerful case can be made out for saying that the doctrine of justification arose out of the Galatian debate, and that Paul first propounded it not to answer the question 'How can I find a gracious God?' but to answer the more immediate question, 'How can Jews and Gentiles live together in one community?' Jews were restricted in what they could eat and this led to difficulties when it came to table-fellowship with Gentile Christians. Must such Gentiles be circumcised and keep the Law in order to preserve the unity and single fellowship of the church? Or are there two ways to Christ, one fully within Judaism, acknowledging him as Messiah and Lord without jettisoning the Law, and one by the direct route of faith? In short, must Gentiles become Christians only through a Jewish door? Galatians, the first letter to deal with justification at length, is directed to community questions of this character, as Chap. 2 in particular shows. The issue is fellowship between different sections of the community and not, or at least not primarily, the individual's restoration to right relationship with God.

Paul's straightforward answer is that Gentiles need not and *must* not become circumcised in order to be Christians. To be in Christ is to be in a new creation in which circumcision and uncircumcision are irrelevant (Gal. 6: 15). Yet while the argument begins and ends with the community problem, Paul's handling of it does bring in the question of the individual's relation to God. The trouble with insisting on circumcision and the Law is that it removes Christ from the centre and displaces faith as the sole requirement on the human side. Demanding that Gentile converts be circumcised implies that this too is necessary for salvation. When we read in Gal. 3: 10 that 'all who rely on works of the law are under a curse', we may ask, 'Rely on them for what?' Not just for being a good member of the community, for something more personal is at stake. Indeed the argument in Chap. 2 moves from community relations (up to v. 14) to the individual's relationship with God through Christ (vv. 16–21).

According to v. 16, we know 'that a man is not justified by works of the law but through faith in Jesus Christ'. If acceptance with God comes about only through Jesus Christ and faith in him, then it does not come about by circumcision and consequent Torah-observance. Since Paul believes that faith in Christ is not only the necessary but also the sufficient condition for acceptance, even something as holy as the Law cannot be imposed as a further condition, hence 5: 4: 'You are severed from Christ, you who would be justified by the law; you have fallen away from grace.' Those who want Gentiles to accept circumcision and the Law in addition to having faith in Christ are really dethroning him, and proposing not an addition to faith but a substitute for it. This is why Gentiles not only need not but must not be circumcised.

In Galatians, then, the community issue leads straight into the issue of the way to God. In Romans too, though the focus may at first sight appear more individual than corporate, in fact the two aspects are inextricably linked. There is a good case for seeing Rom. 1: 16 — 3: 20 as aiming to demonstrate not so much the sinfulness of every single individual as that sinfulness is endemic among all peoples, Jews as much as Gentiles. Rom. 9–11 with its pre-occupation with the relationship between church and synagogue, historical Israel and Christian community, also shows that the letter is at least as much about who are the people of God as about how the individual can be accepted by God. In Romans, then, the dire situation of human sinfulness can be resolved for individuals and for communities only by Christ, who makes possible the free acceptance of those who put their trust in him (Rom. 3: 23f).

Paul sees all this as nothing essentially new. It is as old as Abraham, and now endorsed and fulfilled by Christ (Rom. 4 and Gal. 3). Abraham was counted acceptable to God because he believed the promise of his fatherhood through Isaac of a vast multitude (Gen. 15: 6), and this was before he was circumcised. It is and always was the way of faith that God requires, not the way of circumcision or the Law-obedience which it represents and initiates.

The sacrificial death of Christ

Reconciliation, redemption, and justification all lead us to the cross (see, for example, Rom. 3: 24; 5: 10f; Gal. 2: 21). In some way they are brought about by Christ's dying. Of course, sacrificial categories are not the only ones used to talk about the cross: together with the resurrection, it is a battle fought and won by Christ against the infernal powers (Rom. 8: 32–9; cf. Col. 2: 15), a victory which his people share; they also share in his victory over the curse of the Law (Gal. 3: 10–14). Again, Paul's major contribution to the theology of the cross and resurrection is that believers participate in them, and this will be the subject of the next section. Nevertheless, he does on some occasions speak of Christ's dying 'for us' (e.g. 1 Cor. 15: 3; Rom. 4: 25), even though he never elaborates the idea but simply assumes it will be understood. In contrast, dying and rising with Christ is worked into his total theology in some detail. The idea of Christ's dying 'for us' was probably common Christian belief which Paul inherited: certainly both Rom. 3: 25 and 1 Cor. 15: 3 are passages where he is probably quoting traditional material. It is highly unlikely, therefore, that this was a specifically Pauline idea.

The notion of vicarious suffering and death was common enough in contemporary Hellenism for it to come as no problem to Gentile Christians. What was new about the Christian message was that Christ's death was a sacrifice for *all* human sin, that it was of universal effect, that it was God himself who effected it through Christ and was not simply the one who had to be placated, and that it was proclaimed in the expectation of the imminent End of the world. In Judaism too the notion of sacrifice was deeply rooted. The sacrificial system of the Temple was a means, though not the only one, of dealing with sin, and it was inevitable that, as in Heb. 10, the death of Christ should come to be seen as the perfect sacrifice achieving more effectively what the Temple ritual aimed to achieve.

In Rom. 3: 23–6 Paul gives the death of Christ an important place in the process of justification and redemption:

> since all have sinned and fall short of the glory of God, they are justified by his grace as a gift, through the redemption which is in Christ Jesus, whom God put forward as an expiation by his blood, to be received by faith. This was to show God's righteousness, because in his divine forbearance he had passed over former sins; it was to prove at the present time that he himself is righteous and that he justifies him who has faith in Jesus.

This passage comes as Paul's answer to the double dilemma of sin which he has been outlining since 1: 18, its character as guilt and its character as slavery. That answer is God's righteousness (vv. 21f) which is both his saving activity, and a power into which believers are drawn that they too may be righteous. His salvation comes wholly by grace, as a gift, without any deserving (v. 24a), and results in the acceptance of those who desperately need it

(v. 26b). In the process, sins are passed over or forgiven (v. 25b), not because he does not care about them, but because he has a way of dealing with them: his righteousness not only forgives, but also restores true life and goodness (cf. v. 22).

There are several reasons for suspecting that Paul is here using an already traditional statement. One is that there are the sort of awkward grammatical connections one finds when a writer breaks into a quotation, and another is that there are unusual words in vv. 24f in particular, such as 'expiation' in v. 25. In any case, whatever its origin, Paul uses the material with approval. The central question it is used to answer is how can God thus freely and unconditionally forgive sins and restore sinners to fellowship and life without implying that ordinarily sin and righteousness do not matter. His answer is partly, as we have just seen, that he shows how much sin matters by finding a way to deal with it and how much righteousness matters by providing a way to it. The answer is also partly in his presentation of the death of Christ in vv. 24f.

The word translated 'expiation' is *hilastērion*, also sometimes rendered 'propitiation' or even 'mercy-seat'. Propitiation is the action of turning away God's displeasure; it is directed towards God. Expiation is the removal of sin from the sinner, and so is human-directed. The difference between the two lies in their intention and object rather than in what is done. The mercy-seat was the lid of the Ark of the Covenant in the Holy of Holies in the Temple. It was regarded as the special focus of God's presence and of his forgiving of Israel's sins, for it was the location of the ritual on the Day of Atonement when Israel corporately confessed her sins and received divine forgiveness.

Thus the word in v. 25 has been variously held to mean that on the cross God's anger was turned away from humanity by a sacrifice which he found uniquely acceptable (propitiation), that in the cross God found a means of dealing with sin (expiation), and that in the cross there is a focus and a making visible of God's mercy to men and women (mercy-seat). All have found defenders, and it is difficult to be sure which is correct. Part of the difficulty lies in the rarity of Temple-imagery in Paul's writing; it occurs seldom so explicitly as here, and this supports the view that Paul is quoting an already traditional formula. The words 'put forward' in v. 25 may also be technical sacrificial terminology. The question is how the sacrificial language was understood.

The propitiation answer is perhaps the least likely, because although the notion of placating the gods was common in Hellenism, it was not common in Judaism, where the stress was rather on effecting the sinner's cleansing than on changing God's attitude. Further, Paul does not in practice appear to associate the cross with the wrath of God, not even in Rom. 5: 9, where being saved from the wrath *follows* being justified by his blood, and is not what the cross in itself achieves, nor in 1 Thess. 1: 10 where it is the resurrection that delivers from the wrath to come. He never says that the cross was necessary to turn away God's anger.

It is increasingly being suggested that Paul's treatment of the cross owed a good deal also to the idea of the righteous martyr whose death was believed to have a cleansing effect on Israel. In 4 Macc. 17: 22 the death of seven brothers for their Jewish loyalty is so interpreted: '. . . they having become as it were a ransom for the sins of the nation; and through the blood of these righteous men and their expiatory death, the divine providence delivered Israel which had hitherto suffered evil . . .' The word rendered 'expiatory' is *hilastērion*. Although 4 Maccabees is later than Paul, similar ideas are well represented in contemporary literature, and it seems likely that he and other Christians knew of them. Christ's death may thus have been seen as doing more effectively and universally what the deaths of the righteous martyrs did, but the shocking thing is that it is the death of a crucified — and therefore accursed — Messiah. Therefore, behind Rom. 3: 25 may be not only the Temple ritual, but also martyr theology. Other passages about the death of Christ 'for us' may reflect the same influence.

A word may be added about the theory that Paul takes up the idea of the binding of Isaac (Gen. 22), which, although it did not end in the death of Abraham's only and beloved son, was in some Jewish circles regarded as the perfect and archetypal offering because of the willingness to sacrifice even what Abraham held dearest. It was probably not as influential on Paul as the righteous martyr idea, but may lie behind Rom. 8: 32.

Dying and rising with Christ

Although he uses common early Christian tradition about Christ's death 'for us', what he elaborates is the idea of dying and rising *with* Christ. We may seem to have forgotten his understanding of Christ as power, and of new life as entering into that power and so escaping from sin and death. Justification and what we have been saying about the cross have indeed been more concerned with guilt and liability than with liberation from bondage. We have been concentrating on one aspect of sin and so of salvation, but now move to the other, the slavery from which escape is now possible. Some interpreters have argued that there are two kinds of salvation language in Paul, the juristic (especially justification) and the mystical (especially dying with Christ and being in him). There has also sometimes been a stress on one of these over against the other, but Paul himself shows no awareness of any problem. Just as he sees sin under the two aspects of voluntariness and involuntariness, so he sees salvation as providing both a new status, a new relationship, and a new existence, a new way of living. He deals with the two aspects indiscriminately and in juxtaposition.

In leaving the old bondage, men and women need their sins forgiven and their relationship with God put right, but then need to be kept there. Forgiveness was a common enough theme in Judaism, and there were means to it available in repentance, in the Temple ritual, in suffering, and in death. Christ was not needed to introduce it, though of course he was seen as underlining it. The new development is Paul's proclamation of death to the old bondage and entry into the new freedom of God. In Romans, after arguing that justification is by faith and not by Law-observance (Chaps. 3–4), and after talking about reconciliation and the contrasting effects of the two Adams (Chap. 5), he turns in Chap. 6 to the charge that justification by faith strikes at the root of morality. He has indeed already given hints that he is talking about more than a new status, but now he concentrates on the renewal of life that Christ brings. He reacts with astonishment (v. 2) to the suggestion that if God does not accept us on the basis of our moral achievement then it does not matter whether we are moral or immoral. Those who have responded in faith to Christ and so have been justified, have in that very response died to sin and no longer live under its power (vv. 1f).

It is here that we find Paul's only substantial theological treatment of baptism. He can think of it as cleansing (1 Cor. 6: 11) and as coming into the possession of Christ (1 Cor. 1: 12–17), but here he sees it as conveying dying and rising with Christ (Rom. 6: 3f). Of course the details cannot be pressed: the baptized have risen from the water, but not yet from the dead (v. 4), and it is not certain that the total covering of the baptizand by water is in mind as representing death to the old life. However, there is a death with Christ to all the old securities, dominations, and powers (vv. 2–7, 11). The consequence is new life, just as it was for Christ himself, though the full realization of this awaits the resurrection which has happened to Christ but not yet to the believer (vv. 4f, 8f). None the less, believers who have thus died will rise, and meanwhile are to think of themselves as having already in principle entered new life (v. 11). They must see themselves as people who have been transferred from one lordship to another, so that the old person under the lordship of sin no longer exists (vv. 6–8).

Paul goes on to say that if this is so, believers must live accordingly (vv. 12–23). They must submit themselves totally to the new Master, Christ (or righteousness), in place of the old master, sin (vv. 12–14, 16–20). Further, as the end result of sin's domination was death, so the end result of the new domination is eternal life (vv. 21–3). Then in Chap. 7 he compares the widow's freedom from the rule of her husband with the Christian's freedom from the Law, and (vv. 5, 8f, 11) from the sin that exploits the Law. Death liberates from old dominations (the analogy is inexact but the point is clear). He does not envisage absolute freedom, but freedom to serve in the Spirit (v. 6). The service of God that the Law sought at last becomes possible, all other powers having been overcome (Rom. 8: 4, 38f).

We have seen that it is unlikely that the Hellenistic mystery religions provide the background in any crucial way to the dying and rising with Christ idea in Rom. 6. Long ago Albert Schweitzer saw that the controlling idea was rather that the death and resurrection of Christ marked the End of the Age and the beginning of the New, so that dying and rising with Christ means leaving the old with its malign powers, and entering the new under divine power.

If we were right in our interpretation of 'in Christ', it is not surprising that this is placed side by side with dying *with* him, without any apparent awareness of logical incongruity. At the first climax of the key dying and rising passage (Rom. 6: 11) we read: 'So you also must consider yourselves dead to sin and alive to God in Christ Jesus.' The two kinds of expression are mixed also in 1 Cor. 15: 22; 2 Cor. 5: 14, 17, 21. In effect, dying *with* Christ is the way to become *in* Christ, for the first concerns transfer from the old domination, and the second concerns the consequent existence under the new power, Christ. The key is the faith which is response to Christ: by faith one is accepted by God and restored to right relationship; by precisely that same faith one dies to the old securities and goals and powers; and by faith one finds new life, in Christ.

The new life

Life in the new power is eternal, it cannot be destroyed by physical death (Rom. 6: 23). The resurrection remains a future event, though it casts its shadow before it. It is true that in Col. 3: 1 we read: 'If then you have been raised with Christ, seek the things that are above, where Christ is . . .' Yet even here it is evident from elsewhere in the letter that the rising has not yet happened and can be spoken of only by anticipation (see 2: 6, 12). Its present incompleteness is obvious in the life of the Colossians (2: 21f; 3: 5ff). It is in 1 Cor. 15 that Paul moves the focus from the incomplete to the fulfilled, to the life which is no longer anticipated but is realized. The meaning of the resurrection teaching of this chapter is not universally agreed, and the account about to be given is not the only possible one, but is at least plausible.

We begin looking at 1 Cor. 15 by considering the word *sōma*, 'body'. It cannot simply mean the physical body, though of course in other places it can, nor can it simply mean the person, though it probably means that in Rom. 12: 1. Not surprisingly in view of the Hellenistic nature of the Corinthian church, it seems to mean something like 'outward form', or 'embodiment', or perhaps better 'the way in which the person is conveyed and expressed'. In this passage Paul appears to be trying to avoid two opposite traps: the trap of a completely disembodied future life on the one hand, and on the other hand the trap of a future life which is just a continuation of present physical life. The person continues, so there is no question of exchanging one person for another, as if one died and a quite different one rose. Rather, people die in one form, and rise in another, which means that *sōma* cannot mean either 'person' or 'physical body'.

In Paul's day life after death was differently conceived by different groups of people. Some, under Greek influence, thought of a disembodied state, the immortality of the soul. Some may have thought of a strictly physical resurrection, but many Jews thought of a body that was somehow transformed. Paul does not entertain the idea of disembodied life after death, sharing as he did the Jewish distaste for this as a form of nakedness (see 2 Cor. 5: 1–4). Some people in Corinth may have taken the word 'resurrection' too literally, thought of it in crassly physical fashion, and therefore rejected it. Conceivably they are those 'who did not believe in the resurrection' of 1 Cor. 15: 12.

Paul avoids both extremes and argues for a resurrection of the whole person, involving embodiment but not physical embodiment. There are different kinds of embodiment (vv. 35–44), and the resurrection kind differs from the kind that dies, vv. 42b–44:

What is sown is perishable, what is raised is imperishable. It is sown in dishonour, it is raised in glory. It is sown in weakness, it is raised in power. It is sown a physical body, it is raised a spiritual body. If there is a physical body, there is also a spiritual body.

Clearly he means that the stuff of the embodiment is different, and not physical in the ordinary sense. At the same time, the word 'spiritual' (*pneumatikon*) indicates that it is God-given, and not a natural possibility. It is provided by God for the new conditions which are not those of flesh and blood, but of the new life with him. No doubt this leaves many metaphysical questions unanswered, but it says what Paul wants said.

Yet all this lies in the future, except that life in the Spirit can and must precede life in the spiritual *sōma* (see Rom. 8: 1–17: Gal. 5: 16–25). To be in Christ (now) is also to be in the Spirit (now), and the opposite of being in the *sarx*. Indeed the presence and power of the Spirit, the *arrabōn* (see p. 70), is the guarantee of life in the New Age which still lies in the future but is already enjoyed here and now. Such life in the Spirit bears fruit, as we have seen, in the church-orientated gifts mentioned in 1 Cor. 12: 4–11, 28–30, and in the ethical fruits of Gal. 5: 22f. The Spirit is the giver of life (Gal. 5: 25), and the indispensable mark of being Christian (Rom. 8: 9), as well as the power under which believers live (1 Cor. 2: 4; Rom. 15: 13). As the Spirit of freedom, he liberates from other powers like sin and death (Rom. 8: 2) and Law (Gal. 5: 18).

To be in God's power-sphere, in his Spirit, is not just, however, a new subjection, for Christians obey not as slaves but as sons who can call God 'Abba', Father (see p. 43, Gal. 4: 5–7; Rom. 8: 14–17). The Spirit turns ordinary men and woman into children of God who live in his power and bear his fruit, adopted children, whose adoption now anticipates the full adoption of the future (compare Rom. 8: 15 with v. 23).

As a postscript, we may at this point ask about the relation of the Holy Spirit who gives new life, to the human spirit. Spirit for Paul, as for Judaism generally, was the divine especially in its communication with and action upon the human. Therefore it is possible that it ought always or nearly always to have a capital S, remembering that as Greek was written in capital letters in Paul's day it was not possible to distinguish between 'Spirit' and 'spirit'. All his letters were capitals. On occasions, however, 'spirit' does seem to be merely a constituent part of the human being, as in 1 Thess. 5: 23: 'may your spirit and soul and body be kept sound and blameless at the coming of our Lord Jesus Christ.' Even here questions arise about the difference between spirit (*pneuma*) and soul (*psuchē*), and the relation between the human spirit and the divine Spirit (v. 19). A Hellenistic explanation could be that spirit is a very fine heavenly substance and that 'my spirit' is simply the divine in me, part of and having the same character as the divine Spirit. For Jewish tradition, on the other hand, and for Paul, Spirit is above all the divine activity, so how can he speak of the human spirit? Do believers have two spirits, one divine and one human?

In fact, on most occasions Spirit in Paul is the divine Spirit, and when he speaks of 'my' or 'your' spirit, he means the divine life as it exists in us. My spirit is not part of my make-up, not my possession, but the Holy Spirit at work in me. It is called mine because it is the basis of my existence, not because it has ceased to be God's. Sometimes its origin outside the person is stressed, as when it is in contrast with mind (1 Cor. 14: 14), or when the Christian's total dependence on God is in the foreground (as in Rom. 8: 10f, where there is no distinction between 'your spirits' in v. 10 and 'his Spirit which dwells in you' in v. 11). The fact that my spirit is in fact God's Spirit shows that Christian existence is based in the life of God and not in ordinary human possibility. It also explains the difficulty of knowing where to put a capital letter, and accounts for Paul's curious habit of using 'your spirit' in a greeting (Gal. 6: 18; Phil. 4: 23; Philem. 25), where the first word is plural and the second singular. He is reminding them that though they are many, there is only one Spirit in them all, binding them together.

The new righteousness

Although it is sometimes suggested that Paul can use 'justification' and 'righteousness' interchangeably, this is probably wrong. Justification means restoration to relationship; righteousness is how one lives within that restored relationship, it denotes the new life of the redeemed, including their moral renewal. Like justification, it is not by anything but by faith, and through Christ (Rom. 9: 30 — 10: 4). The continuing life of the believer is thus rooted and grounded in God, and in his righteousness, for the righteousness of God (e.g. Rom. 1: 17) is a power which not only justifies sinners and restores them to acceptance with him, but also keeps them there and makes them righteous.

This new righteousness is not a possession and does not derive from one's own resources. On the contrary it exists only so long as faith exists and only so long as one is in Christ (see 1 Cor. 1: 30; 2 Cor. 5: 21; Phil. 1: 11; 3: 9; see also Eph. 4: 24 and perhaps 5: 9; 6: 14). He has become our righteousness and in him we come to God's righteousness, depending entirely on faith. It thus follows justification, and leads on to new life, as we see in Gal. 2: 20f:

> I have been crucified with Christ; it is no longer I who live, but Christ who lives in me; and the life I now live in the flesh I live by faith in the Son of God who loved me and gave himself for me. I do not nullify the grace of God; for if righteousness (RSV justification) were through the law, then Christ died to no purpose.

It is better to translate *dikaiosunē* here as 'righteousness' in line with its usual meaning in Jewish literature. Paul has indeed in Gal. 2: 15ff been talking about justification, using the verb *dikaioō*, but by v. 20 he has moved on from that to the consequent new life, and is arguing that righteousness, like justification, is by faith, in Christ.

In our discussion of the problem of sin we found that Paul sees it as both wrong relationship and alien domination. When he links justification and righteousness by faith, as here and in other passages like Rom. 5: 18–21 and 9: 30 — 10: 10, he is attacking both aspects of the problem. We again find that Paul has no difficulty in mixing his talk about acceptance ('juristic') and about new being ('mystical': a rather inapt term). The mixing here is by the juxtaposition of words which in Greek — and in French and German though not in English — have the same root. Being in Christ means new relationship, but it also means new life morally and in every way.

Conclusion

Everything that controls the life of the natural man or woman has been overcome by Christ and his Spirit, by a life that is stronger than death and a righteousness that is stronger than sin. Sin is forgiven, a right relationship with God is restored, and life is lived in a new sphere of directing and enabling power. The final outcome is not to be absorbed into God but to be with him and with Christ (1 Thess. 4: 13–17; Phil. 1: 23). In all this Christ's death is central, not only in the traditional sacrificial sense, but much more as something in which believers participate so that his death because of sin is appropriated and shared in as their death to sin (Rom. 6: 10f). They have died with him to sin, and already provisionally know something of the life they will enjoy when all God's purposes are consummated through Christ.

Perhaps the most telling passage for this understanding of the cross and of the Christian's transfer from one power to another is 2 Cor. 5: 11–21, where Paul talks about reconciliation to God and about the new being, the new creation, all in one breath. Christ's death is not simply external to us, v. 14: 'For the love of Christ controls us, because we are convinced that one has died for all; therefore all have died.' Christ has not died *instead of* us, but to enable us to die, just as he rose to enable us to rise (1 Cor. 15: 22; 2 Cor. 5: 15).

6

Christ and the Law

We have several times been brought up against the problem of
the Law, which is both something from whose sway Christians
are delivered, and also something that remains 'holy and just and
good' (Rom. 7: 12, cf. v. 4). As a Jew, Paul read the Old
Testament and could hardly ignore the Law's central place in the
life of Israel, yet his theological scheme of things appears to leave
it almost no place. His concern was far from arising only from
theoretical factors. The confrontation at Antioch (see on
Justification in Chap. 6) exposes practical problems, and the issue
of the relation of the church to Israel (see Chap. 4) was made
concrete in the problem of relating Christians to the neighbouring
synagogue. Yet Paul's attempts to deal with the problem were
grounded in theology, and we now try to draw together what he
says about it.

The Law cannot save

The view has long prevailed that what Paul really objected to was
contemporary Judaism's use of the Law to gain acceptance with
God: 'justification by works'. Much has been made of the piling
up of merits to 'buy' a person's way to God's favour and to
heaven. It is now clear that this is a travesty of Palestinian
Judaism, which did *not* suppose that people could earn God's ✗
favour. On the contrary, his favour was freely given, without any
deserving on Israel's part, in election and covenant. The role of
the Law was to show the nation how to live within that covenant
in order to maintain (not create!) the relation to Yahweh. Its role
was *not* to enable people to find a place within the community
of Israel in the first place. Moreover, perfect obedience was not

expected, and there were means of atonement and forgiveness for the inevitable lapses, so long as there was a fundamental intention to be within God's people, and his covenant. Lack of that intention amounted to apostasy, and this did put one outside the covenant and so outside the realm of salvation. Nevertheless, those who genuinely tried to live by the Law and made atonement for their failures, remained within Israel and had the assurance of a place in the life to come. Merits and demerits had their effect on individual and national fortunes *in the present life*, and were not calculated by God as qualifications or disqualifications for the life of heaven. All this has been sharply underlined by E. P. Sanders in *Paul and Palestinian Judaism*, 1977. He has rendered out of date a good deal that has customarily been said about the Judaism contemporary with Paul.

If this is correct, it leaves us with the problem of how to explain Paul's attack in passages like Gal. 2: 16 and Rom. 3: 28. Who thought justification was by works of the Law? Some certainly did: 'You are severed from Christ, you who would be justified by the law; you have fallen away from grace' (Gal. 5: 4). Those who believed in justification by works of the Law were important enough to provoke an extensive and energetic response from Paul, so who were they, if they were not Palestinian Jews?

The first possibility is that what we have just been saying is incorrect, that contemporary Judaism did believe in earning God's favour, and that our sources (which in their present form are mostly several centuries after Paul) have given a misleading picture. This is unlikely because of the volume of material, and because what can be dated near Paul's time does not on the whole allow such a possibility.

The second possibility takes up the words 'on the whole' of our previous sentence. Was there one strand of Judaism which, unlike the rest, did believe in earning God's favour? This one strand could be represented by 2 Esdras and the Syriac Apocalypse of Baruch (*2 Apoc. Bar.*), where a wealth of good works and observing the commandments are essential for salvation. Indeed in 2 Esdras it is doubted whether more than a tiny minority will be meritorious enough to be saved (see 9: 15f). Do these two books represent a tradition that Paul knew, even though it was untypical of Judaism in general? This possibility cannot be entirely disregarded, but a great difficulty is that both books are dated after the fall of Jerusalem (AD 70), and may therefore reflect an increased pessimism and failure of nerve, not to mention an oppressive sense of the sin which must have brought about such a shocking disaster. We cannot lightly project this pessimism, and this view that merits obtain salvation, back to the time of Paul. Moreover, Paul's attacks on the Law do not seem to arise from despair about its efficacy for more than a tiny minority, so much as from his conviction that God's way is different, that of grace and faith.

A third possibility is that Paul attacked not Palestinian Judaism but the Judaism of the Dispersion. Some distinguished names have held this view, and some still do. What is the evidence for it? We are in some difficulty, because we have few sources for Dispersion Judaism, and we do not know how representative of the whole they are, and because what we do have seem not particularly prone to the view that good deeds earn God's favour. Philo is not, for example, nor is the Wisdom of Solomon. Some have argued that the Septuagint was more inclined to this view than the Hebrew Bible, that because its appeal was intentionally more universal it tended to present Judaism as a moral Law and to obscure the covenant perspective, in which the Law was God's guidance to a people adopted by grace. This 'moralism' of the Septuagint could conceivably solve our problem of reconciling Paul's attacks with what we know of Palestinian Judaism; even if Paul himself was a Palestinian Jew, perhaps his opponents were distorted in their Judaism by the supposed moralism of the Septuagint. Yet why do so few scholars follow this way out of the problem? There are three considerations here:

(a) From what Paul says about himself (e.g. in Phil. 3: 4–6), we have every reason to suppose that his matrix was Palestinian Judaism. Even if he also came to know a different Judaism in the wider world, he would remain well aware of the intimate relation of Law to covenant, of obligation to gracious gift; he had only to listen to Deuteronomy. Moreover, we have seen from

Gal. 4 that it is not only the Law, it is also the covenant as usually understood, that he is unhappy about. His attack on the Jewish position cannot arise from ignorance of it in its Palestinian form.

(b) From a battery of learned works in recent years, notably Martin Hengel's *Judaism and Hellenism*, it is apparent that a sharp distinction between Palestinian and Hellenistic Judaism cannot be sustained. Not only was Dispersion Judaism probably often conservative and quite unlike that of Philo, but Palestinian Judaism was considerably penetrated by Hellenism. The whole picture is too mixed and confused for us to be able confidently to place Paul in one kind of Judaism rather than another.

(c) A great deal of exegetical work in recent years has shown that Paul's meaning is repeatedly illuminated by Rabbinic Judaism. If we have to choose between Palestinian and Dispersion Judaism as his milieu, then the case for the former is overwhelming.

The fourth possible explanation of Paul's attack on those who thought justification was by works of the law is very different. Paul's opponents may have been Judaising Christians who were not Jews at all. Even in Galatians Paul does not in so many words accuse Jews of being addicted to justification by works of the Law, and it is quite possible that his opponents were *Gentile* Christians who had begun to explore their adopted heritage and found there a greater emphasis on keeping the Torah which they now proposed to import into the church. In doing so, they distorted it, and made it what it had not been in Judaism, a pre-requisite for salvation. If, on the other hand, they were Jewish Christians, their insistence on the Law was to enable them to live in one community with Gentile Christians without betraying their heritage. Unfortunately, this inevitably led to distortion, for the Gentiles took them to be insisting on a new pre-requisite for salvation. Either way, Paul was violently opposed to any requirement other than faith in Christ and rejected the proposal to practise circumcision and keep the Law. That the Law's traditional role was misunderstood by the Galatians is suggested by Paul's need to explain that circumcision cannot be isolated but entails keeping the whole Law (Gal. 5: 3; does Rom. 2: 25f indicate the same faulty understanding in Rome?). Moreover, in Gal. 3: 10 he quotes the Septuagint of Deut. 27: 26, ' "Cursed be every one who does not abide by all things written in the book of the law, and do them." ' The Hebrew reads less rigorously, ' "Cursed be he who does not confirm the words of this law by doing them." ' The usual Rabbinic interpretation was that a right intention was required, and Paul may take the more exacting view in order to stress that keeping the Law was wide-ranging and not to be lightly undertaken.

None of these possibilities is entirely convincing. What is quite clear, however, is that the greatest objection to the Law is that it tends to be a rival to Christ (see again Gal. 5: 4: adhering to the Law for justification means severance from Christ). Paul encountered Christ before he saw anything wrong in contemporary Judaism, and it is because he believes that Christ exposes and then solves the human dilemma that he can dismiss all other ways that claim to lead to life.

Then what place for the Law?

In examining this question, perhaps more than any other, we must remember the interaction between the particular circumstances in which a given letter was written, and Paul's coherent point of view which continued throughout. He has neither a series of unrelated positions nor a habit of forging ahead unaffected by the specific problems being faced. As a rule, Galatians is more negative about the Law than Romans.

1. *The Law reveals sin*. This is a positive function, and may be what is meant in Gal. 3: 22: 'But the scripture consigned all things to sin . . .' Certainly in Rom. 7:7 it is the Law that makes people aware of sin. Sin as a state of radical wrongness cannot be perceived as such until there is a specific command which is either broken or is a means of revealing a hitherto unrecognized attitude. This is sharply seen in the case of the Tenth Commandment (Rom. 7: 7b): 'I should not have known what it is to covet if the law had not said. "You shall not covet." ' Again, the Law enables sin to be seen in its true nature as disobedience to God (Rom. 7: 13).

It works rather like a poultice, bringing to the surface hidden poison which can thus be recognized and dealt with. Perhaps Rom. 5: 20, 'Law came in, to increase the trespass . . .' is to be taken in this way. It increased not latent sin, but actual transgression. Rom. 7 as a whole shows that this is a good and beneficent function of the Law (see also Rom. 3: 20 and perhaps Gal. 3: 19).

2. *The Law points forward to Christ*. This too is a wholly good function. The book of the Law, the Pentateuch, is as much tradition as command, and as such is prophetic of Christ in showing the cruciality of faith: this is the point of Paul's Abraham argument in Gal. 3 and Rom. 4. In Rom. 3: 31, before introducing Abraham and after showing that people are justified by faith and not by works of the Law, he asks, 'Do we then overthrow the law by this faith? By no means! On the contrary, we uphold the law.' He means that the Law itself (here, the book of Genesis) says just what he says. In it, too, faith is the way to God's acceptance, so the Pauline teaching is no innovation but rather celebrates the fulfilment of the ancient promise. Unlike the second century Marcion, Paul does not wish to jettison the sacred books of Judaism, least of all the Pentateuch. Because of its prophetic function he can retain Old Testament scripture while rejecting the Law's sway over Christians. We have seen that in Gal. 3 and 4 the Mount Sinai covenant and the Law are either a diversion from or a perversion of the faith-promise covenant with Abraham, but that this conclusion is reached not by ignoring the Old Testament but by reinterpreting it. We have also seen that in 2 Cor. 3: 12–17 the Mosaic covenant can point to Christ when read or heard by those who turn to him and his Spirit. It is Israel's mistake to hear through a veil.

3. *The Law is temporary*. In Gal. 3 Paul argues that justification always was by faith, and that the coming of the Law centuries after the promise to Abraham does not nullify the faith-promise character of the covenant (v. 17). He then says, vv. 19–25,

Why then the law? It was added because of transgressions, till the offspring should come to whom the promise had been made; and it was ordained by angels through an intermediary. Now an intermediary implies more than one; but God is one. Is the law then against the promises of God? Certainly not; for if a law had been given which could make alive, then righteousness would indeed be by the law. But the scripture consigned all things to sin, that what was promised to faith in Jesus Christ might be given to those who believe. Now before faith came, we were confined under the law, kept under constraint until faith should be revealed. So that the law was our custodian until Christ came, that we might be justified by faith. But now that faith has come, we are no longer under a custodian.

Some parts of this passage suggest that the Law was a temporary hindrance to be removed, but on the whole it indicates a positive preparation for Christ and the fulfilment of the promise. Although the latter predominates and is probably to be allowed to shape our understanding of the whole, we must take account of the negative statements.

'Added because of transgressions' (v. 19) may reflect the tradition that the original Law given to Moses on Sinai was cancelled because of Israel's apostasy during the golden calf incident, and that he then received a second Law which thus does not represent God's original intention for humanity. Moreover, 'angels' and 'an intermediary' (v. 19) may reflect a tradition that this second Law did not come directly from God but through divine agents. In most Jewish thinking this would not make it less binding or authoritative, but would indicate the proper channels of communication through which it came. Paul, however, may be hinting that it is as much the work of angels as of God. The mention of an intermediary in any case points to only indirect commerce with God.

However, we ought not to push the matter too far. It is clear from v. 22 that the Law's function was to make people aware of sin, and so ready for the liberating message of Christ that was the fulfilment of the promise to Abraham. When he says in v. 21

that the Law is not against the promise of God, he means that it cannot destroy the fundamental datum that righteousness is by faith, nor was it meant to, for Law was not intended to 'make alive', but to keep Israel under restraint until Christ should come. The rather negative statements in v. 19 are meant to indicate that the Law is somehow on a lower level of revelation than the promise. In fact, it is God's temporary dispensation not his final word.

In vv. 23–5 Paul talks about the restraining effect of the Law, and the most natural meaning of this is that it restrains sin and stops it from getting out of hand until the coming of the final solution, Christ. A good deal of discussion centres on the meaning of 'custodian' in vv. 24f. The Greek is *paidagōgos*, and means a slave who was not a schoolmaster (as the King James Version wrongly has it), but the person deputed by a father to keep his child in order while very young, and then to escort him to and from school when the time came. He did not take part in the child's education. Although the *paidagōgos* could stand for lack of freedom under the Law, so that Christ's coming enables people to escape from the custodian and emerge as sons and daughters (v. 26), it could also represent the divine preservation until that coming. This would mean that the Law had a strictly temporary but divinely given function of preparing people for Christ and for faith, perhaps in the sense of exposing transgressions and so the need for life (v. 22).

4. *The law is a power from which people are delivered*. We saw this in Chapter 5. It is particularly clear in Galatians (see 2: 19; 3: 13; 4: 5, 8–10, 21–31; 5: 1, 18). The *paidagōgos* passage suggests that to persist in living under the Law in the new day of faith and freedom is anachronistic bondage, and in the Hagar-Sarah allegory, Mount Sinai and what it represents constitute not just a turning away from the Abrahamic covenant, but a slavery. Even in Romans with its more measured attitude, Christians have died to the Law and are set free (7: 1–6). Now if we had only Galatians, we could argue that for Paul the Law is to be rejected for Christians without qualification. In Romans,

however, and in 2 Corinthians, the position is more complex and
it is not immediately obvious exactly what Christians have died
to: the Law in itself, or the misuse of the Law?

Some scholars, like C. E. B. Cranfield in his notable
commentary on Romans, have argued that Paul rejects only the
Law's misuse for justification by works. The Law as divine
guidance stands, in the church as of old. All Paul's negative
remarks about it are in connection with justification and only with
that. When he says (Rom. 10: 4) 'For Christ is the end of the law,
that every one who has faith may be justified' he does not mean
that Christ brings the Law to a termination, but to a fulfilment.
'End' (*telos*) can have both meanings. Christ is what the Law is
really about, its fulfilment, not its termination. The Law is God-
given and holy (Rom. 7: 12; 9: 4) and spiritual (Rom. 7: 14); it
finds its true meaning and goal in Christ, who shows that it is
not for justification, but to provide a pattern of life.

For some passages this view of the matter will do. Gal. 3 and
Rom. 4 do see Christ as the fulfilment of the promises contained
in the Law. In Rom. 9: 30 — 10: 4, however, Paul has been talking
neither about this nor about justification, but about how to find
righteousness, that renewal of life and conduct desired by God.
The logic of the passage appears to imply that, because this is
by faith and not by the Law, Christ is in every sense the end of
the Law for those who believe in him.

There are further serious difficulties in thinking that only for
purposes of justification is the Law abrogated, here and elsewhere.
First, even if *telos* in Rom. 10: 4 does mean 'goal', some sort of
termination is involved, for one who has reached a goal no longer
travels the road. Secondly, the *paidagōgos* passage in Gal. 3
implies that the Law's time is over, however valuable it has been.
Now Paul cannot mean the time of self-justification, for the
discussion about Abraham in Gal. 3: 6–18 shows there never was
such a time. He must mean that the time of the Law as such is
over. Thirdly, when he deals with such crucial matters as
circumcision (Galatians generally; Rom. 3: 30; 4: 9ff), the sabbath
(Rom. 14: 5; cf. Col. 2: 16), and food regulations (Rom. 14–15;
1 Cor. 8, 10), despite the fact that on them all the Law speaks

quite unequivocally, he proceeds to ignore it. Fourthly, in facing ethical problems very seriously and in a far from libertine fashion, as in 1 Corinthians, he fails to cite the Law. The only clear exceptions to this general rule are 1 Cor. 9: 8ff, where he defends his right to material support from his churches partly by quoting Deut. 25: 4, and 1 Cor. 14: 34, but this is widely thought to be a marginal gloss that has crept into the text. Elsewhere the Law is not appealed to for answers, even to the question of incest (1 Cor. 5: 1), where common decency is invoked instead.

Naturally, this rejection of the Law is not a rejection of its diagnostic or prophetic roles, nor is it a rejection of everything *in* the law. Nevertheless what is accepted is because of Christ, not because it is in the Law. No one can serve two masters; for Paul, serving Christ means freedom from the rule of the Law. There is indeed a law of Christ and a law of the Spirit (Rom. 8: 2; Gal. 6: 2), but in both cases what is meant is a rule or regime, not a new code or a renewal of the old one. The nearest he comes to being positive about the Law's role for Christians is when he speaks of love of neighbour as the fulfilling of the Law (Gal. 5: 14; Rom. 13: 8–10), and when he says that those who walk by the Spirit fulfil the Law's requirement (Rom. 8: 4). In all these instances, however, the controlling factor is not the Law but the new life in Christ and his Spirit, and he is talking about the divine intention behind the Law, not the Law itself. He cannot mean, for instance, that loving one's neighbour literally fulfils, in the sense of carrying out, the command to be circumcised.

5. *The Law causes sin*, and does not just expose it. It is difficult to avoid this conclusion from Rom. 7. Our sinful passions were 'aroused by the law' (v. 5), and

> . . . sin, finding opportunity in the commandment, wrought in me all kinds of covetousness. Apart from the law sin lies dead. I was once alive apart from the law, but when the commandment came, sin revived and I died. The very commandment which promised life proved to be death to me.

For sin, finding opportunity in the commandment, deceived
me and by it killed me (vv. 8–11).

All this is very hard to comprehend, especially as Paul proceeds
to say (v. 12) that in itself the Law is holy.

To some extent the negative statements in this passage can be
explained by the poultice effect we have already talked about (see
especially v. 7). By making a concrete command, the Law draws
to the surface latent rebelliousness, and its initial result is to
increase overt transgression. I may be unconsciously covetous,
and the command against coveting makes me aware of my state
and aware that some of my actions, as well as my feelings, arise
from it. This explanation is supported by 7: 13: 'Did that which
is good, then bring death to me? By no means! It was sin, working
death in me through what is good, in order that sin might be
shown to be sin, and through the commandment might become
sinful beyond measure.' Most of the statements in Rom. 7 about
the Law's propensity to cause sin can be explained in this way
(cf. also Rom. 5: 13, 20). It not only exposes but makes concrete
the inner and implicit sinfulness that marks the prisoner of sin.

Yet at least in 7: 5 there seems to be something more: the Law
actually arouses dormant sinful passions. A strong case can be
made for seeing vv. 7–25 as dominated by one issue, and one
command, that against coveting. Peculiarly in the case of coveting,
the Law makes things worse. It is bad enough to covet, but at
least before one hears the command against it it can be given more
respectable names (such as a passion for fairness, or justified
resentment). After hearing the command, we can no longer take
refuge in euphemisms, yet neither can we stop coveting. We go
on coveting, in full knowledge of what it is, and that is why the
Law makes things worse, not better. In this sense, the Law causes
sin. Such an argument does not work at all well for most
commandments, for example the commandment not to murder,
and we may be going much too far if we understand Paul to be
saying that the Law provokes *all* kinds of sin. In the matter of
coveting, none the less, it does, and thereby its impotence to deal
with thoroughgoing sin is exposed.

This explanation is more satisfactory than supposing that in 7: 5 Paul is talking about contra-suggestibility, for it is not true that when faced with a command we all instinctively want to disobey it (some people are all too suggestible, not contra-suggestible!). Moreover it is certainly preferable to supposing that Paul is talking about the Law's propensity to provoke the sins of pride and self-righteousness, for which there is no warrant in the text or the context. Probably the best alternative explanation is that in his own career, Paul's devotion to the Law led to the sin of persecuting the Christians: Gal. 1: 13f; 1 Cor. 15: 9; Phil. 3: 6, and cf. Gal. 3: 13 for adherence to the Law as preventing the recognition of Jesus as Messiah. However, nothing of this is mentioned in Rom. 7, and it is therefore a less satisfactory explanation of v. 5 than that offered above, i.e. finding the key in the specific sin of covetousness.

At all events, it is clear from Rom. 7 that the Law as a regime is unable to deliver people from sin, and can even make things worse. Christ, on the contrary, can deliver them.

6. *The Law is irrelevant to salvation*. What matters is not whether someone is circumcised and so committed to the Law, but whether that person has faith and therefore life in Christ (Gal. 6: 15; Rom. 3: 30; 4: 11f). For 'neither circumcision counts for anything, nor uncircumcision, but keeping the commandments of God' (1 Cor. 7: 19). This is partly like the statement in Gal. 6: 15 that 'neither circumcision counts for anything nor uncircumcision, but a new creation'. In 1 Corinthians, keeping the commandments is what matters; in Galatians it is a new creation. What commandments are meant in 1 Cor. 7: 19? The obvious answer, the Law, presents two difficulties. First, it is unJewish to separate circumcision from the commandments of which it is both part and sign. Secondly, the context is not about the Law but about being at the Lord's disposal. Therefore, although Paul's heritage as a Law-keeper may intrude at this point, more probably 'keeping the commandments of God' means doing what God wants,

being at his disposal without reservation. The total argument of 1 Cor. 7 supports this view, which if correct means that we have no exception to the Pauline position about the Law's irrelevance to new life in Christ.

As a postscript, we may note the possibility that Paul shared a contemporary view, ascribed especially to apocalyptic circles, that in the messianic kingdom the Law would have no further role. Then, because he believed Jesus was the Messiah, he naturally found no continuing place for the Law, and was not therefore unJewish or disloyal to his past. This matter has not been altogether clarified; although there is some evidence for such a view about the cessation of Torah, there is also evidence for an expectation that the Messiah would renew and reformulate the Torah, which would henceforth be kept as never before. In any case too much cannot be made of the point, for Paul never uses the messiahship of Jesus as a reason for his criticism of the place of the Law. A coherent account of his view of the Law is not easy to give, moreover, because he never writes about it systematically, but also because he himself was perhaps somewhat ambivalent about it. He may have been torn between an inherited and instinctive reverence for the Law as divine revelation, and a Christian conviction that it was now a barrier against yielding centrality to Christ.

Undoubtedly the Law has been moved from the centre. It is not (as most of his Jewish contemporaries would have agreed) the way to salvation. It is also not (and here they did not agree) the way to lead a righteous life. He nowhere says that Jewish Christians must not keep the Law; if Rom. 14–15 aims to reconcile Jewish Christians who observe the sabbath and the food laws with Christians who believe themselves liberated from such observances, then it is noteworthy that he counsels mutual understanding and tolerance. If some continue to keep the Law, it must not be allowed to become a central issue unless they start to demand that others join them, as in Galatia. Once this happens, Christ is dethroned and Paul's theological hackles rise. This is probably why he is much less tolerant of Jewish observances in Galatians than in Romans.

Is morality unimportant?

The Law gave Israel divine guidance for the whole of life. If for Christians it is no longer the key authority, then where do they look for guidance? One possible answer, given even in Paul's lifetime, is that they need not bother: if justification is by faith, people need not be concerned about right and wrong (Rom. 3: 8; 6: 1, 15). In modern times also, justification has been called 'an ethical cul de sac'. However, to say that moral achievement is not the means of acceptance with God is not to say that *outside the justification context* human behaviour is unimportant. On the contrary, justification by faith is part of a whole which involves leaving the old way of being and the old realm and entering a new one. He who is justified by faith dies to the old self, and lives under the authority and power of Christ and the Spirit. In that new realm there is no place for immorality or unrighteousness (Rom. 6: 12–23).

Another aspect of this matter is the vexed question of the relation of justification by faith to judgment by works. There seems to be a way in which Paul does not see these as incompatible. Though we may perhaps exclude Rom. 2: 13 ('For it is not the hearers of the law who are righteous before God, but the doers of the law who will be justified') on the grounds that it depicts not Paul's own view, but that of the Jews whose position he is discussing, there are still passages which do look forward to a judgment according to what people have done. Christians are not immune from the Judgment (Rom. 14: 10); the work of missionaries will be assessed at that Judgment and be approved or rejected, though the missionaries themselves may be saved despite the condemnation of their efforts (1 Cor. 3: 12–15); and there will be divine judgment on Christians who suppose they can indulge in immorality (1 Thess. 4: 6). The sharpest statement is in 2 Cor. 5: 10: 'For we must all appear before the judgment seat of Christ, so that each one may receive good or evil, according to what he has done in the body.'

Although such statements are few and scattered, they cannot be ignored, for while justification is entirely by faith, faith works itself out in love (Gal. 5: 6) and love is always a matter of how one behaves. The proof of the pudding is in the eating: those who have genuinely found acceptance and new life in Christ will show it in their lives. Justification by faith and judgment by how one has lived (never, in Paul, 'by works', which refers to works of the Law) are not seen as incompatible.

Ethics and the nearness of the End

Paul is thus not unconcerned about behaviour. In all his letters, without exception, he enjoins a high morality and a total obedience to God's will. What is the source of this morality and how does one know what God wants? We shall examine Paul's ethical bases and attempt to see them working out by taking concrete examples. There are several overlapping aspects, and what follow are not alternatives but contributions to a total picture.

We have seen that for Paul Christ marks the end of the Old Age and the inbreaking of the New, and that his death and resurrection represent the move from one to the other. Christians live on the edge of the times; Christ will before long return to complete the process, whether or not in Paul's lifetime. Some have considered this imminence to be the controlling factor in Pauline ethics, on the one hand inhibiting the development of a full code of conduct for Christians, and on the other giving a highly provisional flavour to the treatment of particular issues. That is, apart from endorsing conventional morality, he merely gives advice for an interim period, not for an indefinite future.

This is not an adequate account of the matter, but there are two main places where the expectation of an imminent consummation does crucially affect ethical teaching: 1 Thess. 4–5 and 1 Cor. 7. In the former, two consequences flow from the shortness of the time: the importance of holy living, being ready to face Christ as judge (1 Thess. 4: 1–8; 5: 23); and the need for alertness and sobriety (1 Thess. 5: 1–11). More specific consequences of imminence appear in 1 Cor. 7, in the form of new attitudes to possessions, slavery, circumcision, and especially to relations between the sexes.

Marriage

Undeniably in 1 Cor. 7 Paul prefers the single to the married state (vv. 8, 37f). In v. 1 ('Now concerning the matters about which you wrote. It is well for a man not to touch a woman') we probably have a quotation from what the Corinthians had written to him. If there were incipient Gnostic tendencies in Corinth, some probably believed that it did not matter what the body did so long as the inner and divine essential person was untouched. Thus it would be unimportant whether they slept with prostitutes (1 Cor. 6: 12–20). Others, however, would make the alternative Gnostic response of asceticism, repudiating all sex, and it is this that probably lies behind 1 Cor. 7. Paul's reply is that marriage — a full marriage, sex included — may be a second best but is certainly not sinful (vv. 2, 9, 36, 38), and is preferable to remaining single and being unable to control one's desires. In effect, 'If you must marry, do so with a good conscience, but if you need not, don't.' Why does he prefer the single state? Clearly not because sex is sinful: he does not recommend that a couple live together without sex in a 'spiritual marriage'. Such a practice did exist in the early church, and conceivably Paul is talking about it in vv. 36–38. It is also possible that he is talking about a father granting permission to marry to his daughter of marriageable age (the word translated 'betrothed' by RSV in v. 36 is literally 'virgin' or 'young woman'), but most likely he is talking about betrothed couples.

He strongly deprecates abstinence within marriage, except for short periods in order to concentrate on prayer (vv. 5f). Indeed vv. 3–5 strike a blow for true mutuality too little noticed by those who see Paul as the arch male chauvinist. In v. 4 he says that the husband rules over the wife's body, a sentiment with which few in the ancient world would have disagreed, but goes on in a way many would have found objectionable and even incomprehensible (v. 4b): 'Likewise the husband does not rule over his own body, but his wife does.' This idea that conjugal rights are mutual was remarkably radical. Clearly his preference for the unmarried state does not arise from a spirituality that fears or scorns sex.

He does not advocate divorce either, even where one partner is pagan. On the contrary, one Christian partner can sanctify a marriage, so that its children are Christian (vv. 12–14). Divorced people may remarry, but the original spouse only (vv. 10f). Widows may marry Christian men, but are advised to stay as they are (vv. 39f), as always throughout this chapter. As there is no suggestion that one state is holier than the other, why is there this consistent preference for being single?

The answer comes in vv. 17–35, and it is not that celibacy is intrinsically better than marriage, but that as far as possible Christians ought to stay as they were when they became Christians. The time is short, and believers must be detached from all but the vital concern of doing God's will in the brief time left, concentrating on the propagation of the gospel and the consolidation of the new community. What matters is not circumcision, but doing God's will; not slavery, but being free in things of ultimate importance. Mourning, rejoicing, and all dealings with the doomed world become relatively unimportant; in an urgent situation detachment from the non-urgent is essential. So, unless sexual urges become distracting, it is better to be single and unencumbered, able to give full attention to Christ. Marital affection and responsibility, excellent in themselves, may prove rivals to Christ. The negative approach to marriage is thus part of a general attitude and does not spring from a belief in the intrinsic superiority of celibacy. Even the married are to be detached about marriage (v. 29). As we know from vv. 3–5 that this does not mean sexual abstinence, it must mean keeping marital concerns subordinate to those of being Christian in the shortness of the time. It is striking that he ignores what Jews regarded as the main purpose of sex and marriage, the procreation of children, and this is another indication that the time is short, too short for children to be a factor (though of course existing children are mentioned in v. 14). When he refers to his own single state as a model for his readers (v. 7), he must mean the freedom it gives him for Christian service.

He does seem myopic in his view of marriage. His theology is unexceptionable, yet in his insistence that the married are less free for the Lord he fails to entertain the possibility that the married can do some things for him better than the single, give hospitality for instance. Nor does he allow that a couple's commitment to each other need not compete with their commitment to Christ but may be one way of fulfilling it. Yet what he says about marriage, slavery, mourning, and so on, is not for an ongoing future but for an interim. This is the most notable instance where his belief in an imminent End directly affects his ethical teaching.

Ethics in the New Age

Elsewhere another aspect of his eschatology comes to the fore, concentrating not on the nearness of the End but on the fact that Christians already live as people of the New Age. To a degree this is so even in 1 Thess. 4–5, where the demand for holy living rests not only on eschatological imminence but also on the possession of the Spirit (4: 8) and on God's call (4: 7). The Thessalonians already live in the light of the new day (5: 4f, 10). So too in Rom. 12–13 Christians are urged to be conformed to the New Age, not the old: 'Do not be conformed to this world (Greek: 'age') but be transformed by the renewal of your mind, that you may prove what is the will of God, what is good and acceptable and perfect' (12: 2). At the end of Chap. 13, after treating ethical matters, he returns to the shift of the ages, and urges the Romans to live as already belonging to the New Age, in a holy, loving and righteous fashion.

This reflects the view that Christians are here and now people of God's future. Thus in Rom. 12–13 we find a stress on love (12: 9; 13: 8–10) and on living within the new community in such a way that each contributes to the good of all (12: 3–8). Because Pauline ethics belongs to the new being in Christ, the Law cannot be the controlling factor. This is why it is wrong to see justification by faith as an ethical blind alley. Being within the new power means freedom not for sin, but from sin, which is why in Gal. 5 Paul is at pains to show that to be in the Spirit and not under Law is freedom from immorality, not for it. This does not mean that Christians never sin (Paul still needs to give ethical exhortation), rather that they have freedom from the power and inescapability of sin (ethical exhortation is not crying for the moon). The indicative 'we live by the Spirit' needs to be accompanied by the imperative 'let us walk by the Spirit' in Gal. 5: 25, and those who are dead to sin must live as if they were (Rom. 6: 12–14). This results from the peculiar situation of those who belong to the New Age but still live in the old, the tension produced by Pauline eschatology.

He seems to assume (e.g. in Rom. 6) that his readers will know what righteousness means in practice, and that whether from their knowledge of high pagan morality or from their reading of the Old Testament, they will have commonly accepted standards which can fill in the outlines of general moral exhortation. This tacit assumption occasionally becomes explicit, as for example when he tackles a case of incest at Corinth and says that even pagans frown on this sort of thing (1 Cor. 5: 1f). It surfaces again in connection with the question of what head-coverings should be worn at Christian assemblies (1 Cor. 11: 2–15) and — in so far as we can follow the difficult argument — suggests that the established order of society entails a God-Christ-man-woman hierarchy. The wearing of coverings by women and not men confirms this natural order. He appeals to what is 'proper' and 'according to nature' in a way that puzzles us, but presumably made familiar sense to the Corinthians. It should be added that the issue may have been that some women were adopting (masculine) short hair styles, not that they were refusing to wear veils on top of their hair.

Again, the works of the flesh and the fruit of the Spirit in Gal. 5: 19–23 are lists of vices and virtues like those commonly used in Hellenism and Hellenistic Judaism as a means of moral instruction. These lists tend to be conventional, not meant to be exhaustive but representative, so that, for example, the absence of honesty and truthfulness is unimportant. We cannot make deductions from such absences. Each list stands for all bad things and all good things respectively.

Other examples of conventional ethical material, sometimes using a peculiar syntactical construction familiar from Jewish moral teaching, the imperatival participle, are found in 1 Thess. 4: 1–12; 5: 12–22; Rom. 12: 9–21; cf. Col. 3: 1–17. However, even if like other early Christian teachers he uses material that is traditional and similar in form to Jewish and pagan material, his use is always explicitly in the context of being in the Spirit or in Christ (see not only Gal. 5, but also 1 Thess. 4: 1f, 7f; 5: 10, 18; Rom. 12: 1f; and cf. Col. 3: 1–4).

It is sometimes suggested that he uses the imitation of Christ as an ethical basis. This is correct only within strict limits, Christ's willingness to suffer and die as an act of self-giving and love (see 1 Thess. 1: 6; 2: 14; 1 Cor. 4: 16; 11:1). Only in 2 Thess. 3: 7, 9, where authenticity is disputed, is there anything different, and here it is Paul not Christ who is to be imitated in his industry and refusal to be a burden on others. In general, it is not imitation of Christ but dying with him and being in him that has importance for Paul as a basis of ethics.

Love in the community

To be in the New Age, the new creation, is also to be in the new community, the church, and this too provides a basis for ethics. In 1 Cor. 12: 4–11 Paul shows that the community in the Spirit enjoys various manifestations of that Spirit for the common good (v. 7), and then in vv. 12–31 demonstrates the mutual inter-dependence of members of the body and the reversal of the usual standards of honour and status. He completes a list of gifts of ministry by saying (12: 31 — 13: 1ff) that the most important gift of all is love (*agapē*). This love reflects that of Christ who gave himself for the unattractive and the unworthy (Rom. 5: 6ff), and is characterized by giving not by grasping, by caring as much for others as for self. It comes first in the list of the fruit of the Spirit in Gal. 5: 22. In Rom. 13: 8–10, near the end of his account of life transformed and no longer under malign powers, he describes loving one's neighbour as the fulfilment of the Law (see also Gal. 5: 14).

The practical outworking of the centrality of love is seen in striking fashion in 1 Cor. 8 and 10 in connection with 'food offered to idols'. There seem to be three interconnected questions. The first is whether Christians may attend meals within the pagan temple precincts, in a sort of temple restaurant, but not directly connected with a cultic celebration, knowing that the food served will have been used earlier in pagan sacrifice (Chap. 8). Paul's answer (v. 8) is that in principle there is no reason why not. Idols have no real existence, as those with insight realize, and there can therefore be no danger in eating the food. Nevertheless, people who had previously been devotees of the pagan cult might well interpret eating to mean that it was possible to combine the worship of pagan deities with that of the Christian God. In other words, syncretism, a chronic temptation of converts, would seem allowable, v. 7. This would cut at the root of membership of the New Age, so that the 'strong' Christian who knows no such syncretism is implied becomes the means of destroying the faith of his 'weak' brother, vv. 9–13. Therefore we cannot, says Paul, proceed simply on the rightness or the wrongness of eating. We must put the spiritual welfare of our neighbour first, and however harmless such eating may be for us, we avoid it if it will harm others. In short, love is the guiding principle.

The second question is dealt with in Chap. 10: 14–22, and it concerns participation in the actual cult meals of pagan religion. The advice given differs so markedly from that of Chap. 8, and the setting also appears so different, that we are justified in supposing a different question. Now the answer is straightforward: 'you cannot partake of the table of the Lord and the table of demons'. Idols have no real existence, but like many Jews Paul believes demonic forces exploit them, and to share in idol worship is to put oneself under demonic and hostile powers. There is therefore no way in which a Christian can participate in such explicitly pagan occasions (v. 21) and also participate in the eucharist (vv. 14–18).

The third question concerns eating meat bought in the open market, much of which was also probably left over from pagan sacrifices. Paul's advice in this case (Chap. 10: 23–30) is to eat without questioning the history of the meat (vv. 25, 27). Yet if your host explicitly says that it has been offered in sacrifice, do not eat it, presumably because he is trying to test the exclusiveness of your commitment to Christ. Once again, the point is not whether eating is right or wrong in principle, so much as whether the effect on other people will be harmful (10: 31 — 11: 1). Consideration for others, and their existing or potential adherence to Christ, is the guiding rule; in other words, love. There is another instance in Rom. 14–15, where though the problem may not be exactly the same, the tone of the reply is strikingly similar.

In all these passages, Paul is guided not by a rule but by the Spirit in the light of the concrete situation. There is a conviction that in Christ immediate illumination is given on questions of behaviour. This is underlined by the occasional practice of uttering what have been called 'sentences of holy law' in the form 'If someone does x, then he will be y (by God)' or '*God* will x him'. An example is in 1 Cor. 3: 17: 'If anyone destroys God's temple, God will destroy him.' 'God's temple' here is the church. The confident uttering of judgment or anathema betrays a tacit claim to complete and divine authority (see also 1 Cor. 5: 3–5; 14: 38; 16: 22; Gal. 1: 9). God's final judgment is anticipated in his apostle's utterance. These sentences demonstrate Paul's confidence that Christ's Spirit is working and speaking through him.

Social ethics

Everything so far said about Paul's ethics has concerned the individual Christian or the church. It is often said that he has little interest in the state or society at large. The only direct discussion of citizenship is in Rom. 13: 1–7, which is apparently quietist, advising subservience to the ruling authorities, yet there are qualifications. First, this passage comes in the context of a reaffirmation of the End of the Age (compare 12: 1f with 13: 11f); there can be no thought of refashioning social structures which are in the process of passing away. Meanwhile, Christians live anomalously and anachronistically within present society in a quiet and law-abiding fashion as part of their Christian obedience. Secondly, Rom. 13: 1f says that ruling authorities are to be obeyed because they themselves are established by and subordinate to God. What happens when they manifestly are not subordinate and become totalitarian? Paul does not face this question, but later Christians did, and answered that if Christ is Lord, no one else can be, and a state that claimed too much was to be resisted. In Paul's different circumstances, the institution of government seemed divinely provided, and since the only alternative was anarchy, ought to be upheld by Christians.

Here again is the tension between Christian life as belonging to the New Age and as also still existing in the limitations of the Old. A similar case is where Paul talks about women and seems to contradict himself. On the one hand, 'in Christ there is neither male nor female' (Gal. 3: 28); on the other, women are to remain subordinate to men in accordance with the hierarchical structures of the world (1 Cor. 11: 2-16). None the less it is instructive that within the latter passage come vv. 11f, rightly put in parentheses by RSV, showing the tension between the subordinationist system of the world and the principle of new community in Christ: 'Nevertheless, in the Lord woman is not independent of man nor man of woman; for as woman was made from man, so man now is born of woman. And all things are from God.' What I suspect Paul means is that in the Lord there are no distinctions (cf. Gal. 3: 28), but that in the present world there are, and it is in that present world that Christian obedience is to be practised. The established order must be upheld so long as it lasts, but Christians know it is only provisional and that in the New Age its distinctions will disappear.

The same sort of tension emerges in his treatment of slavery: like those between Jews and Gentiles and between men and women, the distinction between slaves and free is declared defunct in Gal. 3: 28. In the present world, however, it plainly is not defunct, doomed though it may be, and Christians meanwhile must live with it (1 Cor. 7: 21-4). To work for the abolition of slavery in such circumstances would have been like tinkering with the engine of a sinking ship. All this is illuminated by the case of the runaway slave Onesimus, whom Paul sends back to his master Philemon (Philem. 12) in accordance with the rules of society. Yet he asks Philemon to receive him back not as a slave but as a brother *in the Lord*, because both are Christians

(Philem. 16). The rules and structures of society are outwardly respected, but inwardly rejected.

This is not quite all we can say about Paul and society, if we recall that for him the church is the forerunner of the future humanity, the new Adam's people, in whom that future is already partially apparent. What he says about the church thus gives us some clues about how he thinks society ought to be. There is to be mutual dependence and the reversal of usual ideas about status and importance (1 Cor. 12: 14–26). There is to be a just distribution of resources according to need (2 Cor. 9). Above all there is to be love, expressed in attitudes and practices (1 Cor. 8, 10). Paul's preoccupation with the collection (Greek *koinōnia*, 'participation') was largely because it aimed to weld together the different parts of the church, and even perhaps to symbolize the ingathering of the Gentiles. Yet the collection also had a more straightforward purpose: it aimed to ensure that the resources of one part of the church were available for the whole church, especially for the poor (see 2 Cor. 8: 1–4; 9; Gal. 2: 10; Rom. 15: 25–7).

So, the state and society remain, but the theological realities of the New Age are already undermining their inequitable, discriminatory, and hierarchical foundations. To change the metaphor, within the old society is a new one, built on quite different foundations of love, equality, and unity.

7

Pauline Christianity in the New Testament and Beyond

Paul was no isolated figure, but the centre of a way of understanding Christianity that was widespread and influential, at least for a time. We turn now to writings, whether or not by Paul himself (and all that we discuss are either definitely not by him, or frequently thought not to be by him), which represent a second wave of Paulinism. We begin, however, with a letter which if it is genuine, is early.

2 Thessalonians

The theological content of this brief epistle is relatively slight, and apart from 2: 1–12 there is little that is not also in 1 Thessalonians. The wording is often so nearly identical that either Paul wrote the second letter while the first was still in his mind, or a follower wrote the second on the model of the first. The aim seems to be to moderate the Thessalonians' feverish expectation of Christ's imminent return by stressing (2: 1–12) the apocalyptic programme to be completed first. Those who have given up earning their living because the End is so near should get back to work and live quietly, watchfully, and diligently, without being a burden on others. Chap. 2: 1–12 is a traditional piece, more full of conventional apocalyptic imagery than we find elsewhere in Paul (though see 1 Thess. 4: 13–17; 5: 1ff; 1 Cor. 15: 51f). We meet expressions like 'the man of lawlessness', 'the son of perdition', 'the mystery of lawlessness', and the notion of 'restraining'. While in 1 Thessalonians, especially Chap. 5, the End is to be sudden and unexpected, in 2 Thess. 2 signs and portents must come first.

None of this represents an advance on Pauline thinking but instead a more cautious time-scale, and a richer use of traditional imagery. The authorship is much disputed, but in any case the letter makes little contribution to Pauline theology.

Colossians

Here the position is quite different. Whether or not Paul wrote it, development within Pauline theology is evident at several points, most clearly in Christology. Although the undisputed letters do show the beginnings of a cosmic Christology (1 Cor. 8: 5f; cf. 2: 8; Phil. 2: 10; see also Christ's victory over the cosmic powers in Rom. 8: 37–9), in Colossians we find a flowering of such ideas, especially in 1: 15–20. Christ's role as mediator of creation is heavily underlined, and in him God is presented in all his fullness. The passage is widely believed to be a hymn which may have originally been Gnostic, or a Palestinian meditation on Wisdom in the light of Prov. 8: 22 and Gen. 1: 1, or a Hellenistic Jewish Wisdom piece, or perhaps most likely of all, a Christian liturgical confession of Christ on the Jewish Wisdom model. At all events, in its present form it is thoroughly Christian, and consists of two strophes, the break coming in the middle of v. 18. We set it out in a form which reflects its probable nature.

15. He is the image of the invisible God, the first-born of all creation;
16. For in him all things were created, in heaven and on earth, visible and invisible, whether thrones or dominions or principalities or authorities
all things were created through him and for him.
17. He is before all things,
and in him all things hold together.
18. He is the head of the body, the church;
he is the beginning, the first-born from the dead,
that in everything he might be pre-eminent.
19. For in him all the fullness of God was pleased to dwell,

20. and through him to reconcile to himself all things,
whether on earth or in heaven,
making peace by the blood of his cross.

Like Wisdom, Christ represents God's action both in creation and in redemption, and most probably it is the exalted Christ that is in mind throughout.

It is precisely because Wisdom seems to be the model that it is difficult to know how to take much of the language. On the face of it, the hymn proclaims the pre-existence of Christ, who as a person was active in both creation and redemption. Yet our knowledge of Wisdom language must make us cautious; it is possible that what is meant is that the same full presence and activity of God evident in Christ's resurrection and reconciling work was also present at the creation, so that what is pre-existent is not Christ in person, but the power of God that came to be active in him. We cannot therefore be sure how far this is a marked advance on earlier Pauline Christology at least in connection with pre-existence. Thus vv. 15–17 are entirely in line with Wisdom talk, and even the expression 'first-born' in v. 15 cannot easily be assumed to denote personal pre-existence, any more than it can be assumed to mean that Christ-Wisdom is part of creation.

In v. 18a Christ is the head of the body, the church. 'Body' may derive from Stoic views of the commonwealth of humanity as a body, and if so they are corrected so that the church stands for the key community. Christ as the head of the body is a new development. In Rom. 12: 4f Christians are one body in Christ. In 1 Cor. 12: 12–31 they are the body of Christ. Until now it has nowhere been said that they are the body of which Christ is the head. It may be because of the transference of Wisdom-cosmos language to Christ-church that this change occurs. The old idea which equates Christ with the body is still present (1: 24), but it is this new one which is striking. Moreover, just as the cosmic Christ idea is found not only in 1: 15–20 but also in 2: 8–10, so Christ as head of the body recurs in 2: 19 and perhaps 3: 15. Of course, other reasons for this development may have existed, the simplest of which is that for Christians to think of themselves as his body without acknowledgement of Christ as Lord or Head, could lead to pretension and pride. This fear may be traced back to 1 Cor. 1–4 and 12: 12–31 and to Paul's attack on Corinthian self-importance.

In v. 19 with its reference to 'fullness' some see a reference to Gnostic powers and emanations derived from but subordinate to God, so that the hymn proclaims that unlike them Christ represents God totally and not partially. Perhaps it is more likely that it means that like Wisdom, Christ represents God in all his fullness, and is God's cosmic presence. However we take the language, we clearly have here a more developed presentation of Christ in his cosmic significance than we have hitherto met.

Like other letters, Colossians talk of the new being in Christ and of dying and rising with him, which it connects with baptism (2: 12), but is less guarded than Romans and 1 Corinthians in seeing resurrection as belonging to the future. In 2: 12f and 3: 1 the Colossians appear to be already raised with Christ, though there is still an 'eschatological reservation' (3: 3f): 'For you have died, and your life is hid with Christ in God. When Christ who is our life appears, then you also will appear with him in glory.' Thus the 'already' of 3: 1 is accompanied by the 'not yet' of 3: 4. Christians are still on the way and have not yet arrived; they therefore need exhortation to live as if they really have died with Christ (2: 6f, 20–3; 3: 1f, 5–25; 4: 1–6). Moreover, resurrection is present only to faith (2: 7, 12). Yet the shift in terminology is remarkable, and one of the things causing doubt about Paul's authorship.

Other developments are less important. Expectation of an imminent End is missing: only 3: 4 explicitly refers to Christ's final disclosure. Yet the shift of the ages, marked as in the undisputed letters by Christ's death and resurrection, pervades the letter. The ethical instruction in Chap. 3 is akin to the catechetical pattern we find in later writings, the so-called *Haustafeln* (or household codes), but is closely tied to the understanding of Christians as belonging to the New Age. Christ's victory over the powers (which here include the Law, 2: 14f) is also the victory of those who die with him (2: 20), so that once again we have the shift of the ages.

These similarities with and differences from the other letters constitute a problem. Some scholars find the explanation of the differences in the heresy which Paul is fighting, probably a species of Jewish Gnosticism which led him to develop new conceptions and word-meanings. Others argue that because the style and vocabulary are not comfortably within the usual Pauline limits, he himself is unlikely to have been the author. Someone else, a disciple or group of disciples, wrote in his name, claiming his authority. For an investigation of these matters, and of the further questions of the date and place of writing, a standard book of New Testament Introduction should be consulted. Whether or not Paul is the author, and we cannot confidently say that he was, Colossians represents development in Pauline thinking.

Ephesians

The position here is complex. In some ways the most magnificent of all the letters, especially in its emphasis on the reconciliation of Jews and Gentiles in Christ, it shows not only development within Pauline thought but divergences from it, in a way that Colossians does not. There is much that is familiar. Indeed there is much that is familiar from Colossians: they are alike in their treatment of the glorious, victorious cosmic Christ (compare Eph. 1: 19b–23 with Col. 1: 15–20), and in their treatment of the new life in Christ after the death of the old (compare Eph. 2: 1–10 and 4: 17–32 with Col. 3: 1–11). There is much moving exhortation, and a very long catechetical section, 5: 1 — 6: 9.

There are also things that compare oddly with other letters. In 1 Cor. 3: 11 Jesus Christ is the church's only foundation, but in Eph. 2: 20f while Christ is the chief cornerstone, the apostles and prophets are associate foundations. In Paul generally the word 'church' (Greek: *ekklēsia*) is used of a particular local church, but in Ephesians it refers without exception to the church universal (1: 22; 3: 10, 21; 5: 23–5, 27, 29, 32). The view of the apostles and (Christian) prophets is thus becoming more reverential, and the universal nature of the church is achieving greater prominence. No one has ever doubted that these developments occurred; what is interesting is that Ephesians demonstrates their existence within the Pauline tradition, see 3: 5 where 'holy apostles and prophets' smacks of veneration.

There is no expression of hope in an imminent return of Christ, not even the vague sort that persists in Col. 3: 4, and in this Ephesians is unique among Pauline letters. There are also small matters in which it stands alone: for example in Col. 1: 20 God reconciled all things to himself through Christ, but in Eph. 2: 16 Christ does the reconciling *to* God; 'mystery' in Eph. 3: 4ff is no longer the revelation of God's ancient but hidden purposes, but the unity of Jew and Gentile in the church (contrast Rom. 16: 25; 1 Cor. 2: 1, 7; Col. 1: 26f; 2: 2; 4: 3). There is very great thoroughness in treating moral questions in Chaps. 4–6, and a concentration on the revelation of God's mystery in Chaps. 1–3, as well as a basing of the command for mutual subjugation in love on a belief in Christ's sacred marriage to his church in 5: 21–33.

So then, there is an increased glorification of Christ, a more universal view of the church, great reverence for its founding fathers, a falling away of the *parousia* hope, not to mention an assumption of the resolution of past controversies so that Jew and Gentile are one in the church. This is surely a late writing, and if Paul is the author, he must have written it at the very end of his life. Unlike all other Pauline letters, it has no greetings, no mention of individuals, nor of the circumstances of the recipients. Yet Paul knew the Ephesians exceptionally well and had spent a great deal of time with them. Perhaps it was a circular letter (the earliest manuscripts omit 'in Ephesus' from 1: 1), as there is nothing in it to tie it to one particular place. The superscription 'To the Ephesians' is, like all New Testament superscriptions, a later addition. It could thus have been sent to several churches, to represent Paul's final, mature reflection on the achievement of Christ, the reality of the new life in him, and the church as a body under him as its head.

More probably Paul did not write it, not only because of its theology, but also because its language and style are strikingly different from Paul's elsewhere. For example, the word for 'heaven' or 'the heavens' occurs five times in Ephesians, but is always a different one from that used in all the other letters; there is no difference in meaning or perceptible reason for the change, and it is just this sort of detail that betrays a different hand in the opinion of many. Numerous tricks of style are different from Paul's, and encourage the supposition that someone is writing in Paul's name presenting his teaching for a new situation. There is also a curious relationship between Ephesians and other letters, especially Colossians, for despite the stylistic differences much of the content of Ephesians is similar to material in the others. This has given rise to the suggestion that Ephesians is a pastiche put together by a disciple of Paul from his letters. Some American and British scholars have further suggested that it was composed when the letters were collected after a period of neglect in order to introduce them to a wider audience. This explains the similarity in content, the theological development, and the differences in style and vocabulary. Ephesians is thus an attempt to provide 'the meaning of Paul for today' in general terms, because it is directed to the whole church, and in developed terms, because it comes from the end of the century. This theory has some fascinating refinements, including a hypothesis that the collector and compiler was Onesimus, but its weakest feature is that it really requires Ephesians to come first in early lists of Pauline epistles. An introduction ought to introduce, and on this theory Ephesians is an introduction to Paul. Unfortunately it never comes first, and despite ingenious attempts to circumvent this objection, it remains a serious drawback.

What nobody doubts is that it was produced, if not by Paul himself then by someone very close to him and his thinking. In large areas it is thoroughly Pauline, and those who think it the product of a Pauline follower or school, do not intend to minimize its significance. On the contrary, it is an important witness to how Pauline thinking developed in the next generation.

The Acts of the Apostles

Not everyone understood Paul. Both in chronology and in theology there are major difficulties in reconciling Acts and the letters. A famous instance where both sorts of difficulty converge is the so-called Apostolic Council of Acts 15: is it the same event as that of Gal. 2? Both concern the question of whether Gentiles need to be circumcised, and in both the answer is that they need not. However, while in Galatians no special requirements are made of Gentile converts, in Acts 15: 20, 29 they are asked to abstain from meat offered to idols, from meat killed by strangling, which thus still contains blood, and from fornication. If Paul was there and agreed, as Acts has it, why does he not quote the decree in dealing with the Galatian demand that Gentile converts be circumcised? Why does he go against it, in writing to the Corinthians (1 Cor. 8 and 10)? More basically, is it credible that the Paul who wrote Galatians would agree to the imposition of these essentially Jewish conditions on his Gentile converts? Chronologically, how do we explain that the 'council' visit to Jerusalem is Paul's third, according to Acts, but only his second according to his own account in Galatians? Some of these difficulties can be removed by supposing Galatians to be a very early letter, though this creates new difficulties and makes others worse (it certainly does not help to explain why Paul does not quote the decree in Rom. 14–15).

This is only one example of the problems in reconciling Acts and the letters. In general it is not a safe guide to Pauline theology. Although it venerates him, devoting more than half its length to him, it never mentions his letter-writing and does not give him full apostolic status. At the crucial point, therefore, it denies him what he strenuously claims (see 1 Cor. 9: 1; 15: 1–10; Gal. 1: 17 etc.). Even when it describes his call, although at first there are hints that it is a meeting with the risen Christ, it becomes clear in Acts 26: 19 that it is a vision and different in kind from the appearances to the disciples (contrast 1 Cor. 15: 1–11).

More important still is that Acts misses the heart of Pauline Christianity, whether because of 'Luke's' limited theological understanding, or because he wrote much later and was simply ignorant of Paul's distinctive ideas. Paul's speeches in Acts may well reflect Lukan rather than Pauline theology. They do centre on Christ, but there is nothing about the new being in Christ, nothing about the transfer from one dominion to another, nothing about the cross as atoning, nothing about dying and rising with him. The Holy Spirit is prominent, but there is almost nothing about life in the Spirit as equivalent to life in Christ; instead, the focus is more on the manifestations of the Spirit in prophetic speech. There is nothing about the church as the body of Christ. The one mention of justification (Acts 13: 38f) certainly approaches the Pauline doctrine, but it has no reference to faith, it may imply that the Law was adequate for justification up to a point, and its phraseology is not characteristically Pauline. Generally Acts has no grasp of the nature of the conflict about the Law nor of Paul's radical solution to it.

Paul in Acts quarrels with Judaism more over resurrection (4: 2; 23: 6) than over the Law. Indeed Acts ascribes to him an astonishingly positive attitude to the latter. He accepts the Jerusalem decree of Acts 15: 20, 29 and commends it as he travels (16: 4), which must mean that he advised Gentiles to abstain from meat containing blood and from meat offered to idols. This is in the face of a quite different attitude to food regulations in 1 Cor. 8, 10 and Rom. 14, 15, where in any case he makes no reference to a decree. Moreover, in Acts Paul has Timothy circumcised (16: 3), participates in Jewish worship and proves his orthodoxy by taking a vow (18: 18; see also 21: 18–26). When on trial in Jerusalem he says that only his preaching the resurrection is responsible for his predicament (23: 6; 26: 5), and that he remains a Pharisee. Of course Acts is enthusiastically aware of the Gentile mission, but it seems unaware of the consequent agony and conflict even in Paul himself, for all is solved by the divine command to Peter (Acts 10, 11), and any problems are readily solved at the Jerusalem Council of Chap. 15.

The Christology of Acts and of Paul in Acts is very simple, being centred on the Messiah who was rejected by sinful men but vindicated by God at the resurrection, in accordance with the scriptures (13: 13–43; 26: 22f). It is more a theology of glory than a theology of the cross. This is puzzling, for it implies a primitive Christology and soteriology, and so an early date; yet the treatment of the Law implies a time when the battle was over and largely forgotten, as does the lack of a strongly future eschatology. The 'natural theology' of Paul's Areopagus speech (17: 22ff) is akin to the attempts of people like Justin Martyr in the Second Century to discover a preparation for Christ in pagan philosophy and religion, and this too suggests a post-Pauline date. Was Acts therefore written by a contemporary who did not understand him, or by a later person who was inadequately informed?

Whoever the author was, he had only a superficial grasp of Paul's thought. We cannot account for the discrepancies by saying that the letters are pastoral and theological writing for established communities, while Acts describes initial missionary preaching and apologetic. The basic theological position would surely survive the change of occasion. We therefore have in Acts, probably from the end of the first century, the product of a part of the Pauline movement stronger on respect than understanding.

The Pastoral Epistles

The same comment can be made about 1 and 2 Timothy and Titus, known collectively as the Pastoral Epistles. Few scholars defend their having been written by Paul as they stand. As their theology is in some ways more like that of Paul in Acts than that of the other letters, it is not surprising that a case has been made for ascribing them to Luke.

The first thing to hit the reader is that, unlike all other letters attributed to Paul, they are greatly interested in structures and offices. Both Timothy and Titus are in charge of churches, in Ephesus and Crete respectively, exercising a control and oversight similar to and derived from Paul's own. In this they are associated with other overseers (Greek: *episkopoi*, 'bishops'): 1 Tim. 3: 1ff; Tit. 1: 7ff. These may or may not be identical with the elders (Greek: *presbuteroi*) who figure in 1 Tim. 5: 1f, 17, 19; Tit. 1: 5. In the first two instances, however, the reference may be not to an office held but to the age of the people concerned, for like 'elder' in English the word can simply mean an older person.

Because they contain so much about offices and structures, the Pastorals have always provided grist for the mills of later churchmen who wish to prove that their own favoured form of church government (e.g. episcopal, or presbyteral) represents the oldest and divinely sanctioned form. Few scholars approve of such exploitation of the Pastorals, partly because of the gaps in our knowledge: no one is sure whether bishops and elders were identical or different, though the prevailing view is that they were identical.

Although we are told that bishops teach (1 Tim. 3: 2; Tit. 1: 9) and that bishops and elders rule (1 Tim. 3: 5; 5: 17), we are told much less about their duties than about the character they need to have. Timothy and Titus appear superior even to the bishops and to have pastoral responsibility for them. There are also 'widows', who appear to be members of an order fulfilling the sort of functions often associated with the deaconess (1 Tim. 5: 9ff). Although we are uncertain about the exact nature of these offices, the letters' recipients clearly were not, and their knowledge could be taken for granted. The structures are established and are not matters for controversy. What matters is the character and piety of those who fill the offices. A good deal of the character requirement of bishops, elders, deacons, and widows is little more than conventional propriety and common sense, for example 1 Tim. 3: 8: 'Deacons likewise must be serious, not double-tongued, not addicted to much wine, not greedy for gain.' Yet it is characteristic that immediately following (v. 9) we read: 'they must hold the mystery of the faith with a clear conscience'. If one dominant note is personal suitability for office, another is the necessity to safeguard the true faith.

This true faith is not merely to be propagated; it must be preserved against corruption from within and attack from without: 1 Tim. 1: 3f, 19; 3: 9, 15; 4: 1, 6f; 6: 10, 12, 14, 20; 2 Tim. 1: 13f; 2: 15, 18; 3: 14–17; 4: 3f; Tit. 1: 9, 13; 2: 1f. This explains the stress on structures and offices, and on the piety of office-holders (there is much about 'piety' and 'godliness' and being 'religious', all representing the Greek *eusebeia* and its cognates, found in the New Testament only in the Pastorals, Acts, and 2 Peter, 22 times in all, 13 of them in the Pastorals). In close accord with this is the frequent note of warning against a heresy whose threat to the church is met not by argument, as usually in Paul, but by denunciation and reliance on defensive measures. These defences consist of holding fast to the tradition, of discipline, and of recognized authority. Much has been written about this heresy, but as so often we must work largely by inference. Some elements are of indeterminate character, some are clearly Jewish (1 Tim. 1: 6f; Tit. 1: 10–16; 3: 9), and some Gnostic (1 Tim. 4: 1–3, 7; perhaps 2 Tim. 3: 1–9; 4: 3f; Tit. 3: 9). A form of Jewish Gnosticism seems to be in view. One very interesting characteristic emerges in 2 Tim. 2: 18, where Hymenaeus and Philetus have erred 'by holding that the resurrection is past already'. This looks like a belief that may also underlie 1 Cor. 15, that those who are enlightened, who 'know', have already entered the life of the future, have nothing important to await, and perhaps are therefore free from the rules and restraints of ordinary life.

The letters' emphasis on building well on foundations already laid doubtless derives from this need to guard against error, and it also reflects a settled situation. The church faces a continuing life in the world: eschatological expectation is still present, and Christians are living in the last days (2 Tim. 3: 1–6 and perhaps 1 Tim. 4: 1f), looking forward to the return of the Lord Jesus Christ (1 Tim. 6: 14f; Tit. 2: 13), but nowhere is it said that this is imminent. Christians must reckon with a future in this world and must live therein decently and acceptably. Unlike 1 Cor. 7, where issues were discussed in the light of the End's nearness, the Pastoral's ethical advice — of which there is a great deal — is pragmatic and conventional, the sort of thing that is true anywhere at any time, and not just for Christians.

The Pastorals have a curiously staccato effect. Nothing is developed and there is no sustained theological argument. Many things are referred to briefly, but there are no themes apart from the need to guard against attacks on the faith. Some passages are theologically weighty, like 1 Tim. 3: 16, the bulk of which is rightly set out in RSV as a credal hymn, with recurring features and a rhythm more evident in Greek than in English:

> Great indeed, we confess, is the mystery of our religion:
> He was manifested in the flesh,
> vindicated in the Spirit,
> > seen by angels,
> preached among the nations,
> believed on in the world,
> > taken up in glory.

For a credal summary, this has odd features: there is no mention of the cross or of the resurrection. There is nothing to embarrass a Gnostic Christian, and it may even be a Gnostic formulation used here either in ignorance and without due reflection on its character, or in a deliberate but rather weak attempt to turn the Gnostics' weapons back on themselves. While there are such interesting theological pieces, and some strongly reminiscent of the Paul of the main letters (like 2 Tim. 1: 8–10; Tit. 3: 3–8a), the characteristic Pauline notes are largely missing.

The debate about the church's relation to Judaism seems in the past, and the letters have more in common with pagan Hellenistic piety than with Jewish. The frequency of *eusebeia* ('religiousness'), a common pagan word for piety, points to this. Little use is made of the Old Testament. The Law is not a problem; indeed it is regarded astonishingly positively: 'Now we know that the Law is good, if anyone uses it lawfully, understanding this, that the Law is not laid down for the just but for the lawless and disobedient, for the ungodly and sinners . . .' (1 Tim. 1: 8–11). For Paul, on the contrary, it is often the *observance* of the Law that is apt to be a problem. Despite this strange attitude, and despite the Jewish elements in the heresy, there is generally little attempt to deal with the Jewish roots of Christianity. The emphasis is rather on living righteously in the Hellenistic world, causing offence to no one, and obeying the secular powers, and on obedience to Christ.

The whole picture is of a settled and established church whose need is for further consolidation. We are, in other words, in the second Christian generation. Few dispute this, and the question is whether we are within Paul's lifetime at its very end, or after his time when his name and authority are invoked to safeguard 'authentic' Christianity. There are strong reasons to suppose that Paul himself was not the author, and for them it is necessary to consult a New Testament Introduction. Here they can be merely listed.

First, if style is indeed as characteristic as a fingerprint, then Paul cannot be the writer. Secondly, it is virtually impossible to fit the chronology required by the Pastorals into what we know from the other letters and from Acts (for example, when did Paul fit in the extended mission to Crete presupposed in Titus?); the only way out is to propose a second wave of missionary activity after Paul's imprisonment in Rome. There is a little evidence of such resumed activity, but it has him going west, not back towards Crete (Titus) or Ephesus (1 and 2 Timothy). Thirdly, the stress on structure and office, and the defensive attitude, point away from Paul and his period. Fourthly, the theology, what there is of it, is not characteristically Paul's despite some Pauline features; almost everything typical of him is absent, and even those features that appear do so in a strangely unPauline manner (e.g. 1 Tim. 1: 8–11 on the Law).

Every one of these reasons can, if with difficulty, be circumvented, but together they form a chain that persuades most investigators that Paul was not the author. Some genuine fragments may have been incorporated, such as the large number of personal notes, though this idea does not gain universal agreement. We have already noted the possibility that the same writer was responsible for both Acts and the Pastorals, and certainly both show a similarly inadequate grasp of Paul's thought. Curiously, non-Pauline authorship enhances rather than diminishes the letters' importance, because it means they give us a valuable glimpse of what happened to Pauline Christianity about the end of the first century.

The second century

In so far as we know it at all, the story after this is fragmentary. About the middle of the second century there arrived in Rome an exotic character named Marcion, who laid such stress on the newness of Christianity as taught by Paul that he could see no connection between the Old Testament God and the Christian God. The first was a God of justice and the second a God of love. The Old Testament and its regulations had nothing whatsoever to do with Christians, who belonged to a stranger God. This stranger God had had no dealings with the world or with humanity; he was not its Creator, nor its Lawgiver, and he was not Israel's covenant God. For no reason other than pure love he sent Jesus Christ to rescue humanity from the creator-God (who was not evil, but merely just) and from the material, corruptible world. Marcion thus went well beyond Paul's distinction between Law and Gospel, to a distinction between the God of the Law and the God of the Gospel.

Marcion made extensive and virtually exclusive use of Paul, believing that Paul alone had preserved the true Christian message. Other Christian writings had become infected by the now obsolete religion of Israel and were thus unusable. Of the gospels, only a carefully expurgated version of Luke was acceptable. Now this rejection of Christianity's Jewish roots did not make him an antinomian libertine; true, the Law had nothing to do with Christians, and to obey it was to resume submission to the God from whom they had been delivered by Christ's death (the purchase price from their previous owner). Yet to be concerned with possessions, food, and sex, was to traffic with the old God and his world, and therefore was to be avoided at all costs. Consequently, Marcionite Christians pursued a strictly ascetic code of behaviour. In all, Marcion grasped the newness in Paul's presentation of Christianity, but failed to grasp its continuity with its Jewish past.

Gnostic Christians also widely used Paul's letters, and this may already be indicated in 2 Pet. 3: 16, where the author says of them: 'There are some things in them hard to understand, which the ignorant and unstable twist to their own destruction, as they do the other scriptures.' Some people were apparently using Paul in an unorthodox way, from the writer's point of view. It is interesting that Paul's letters had gained authoritative status in the church of the second century, when 2 Peter was written, and we see that they were established enough to survive being liked by the Gnostics, who interpreted them in accordance with their ideas.

In Gnostic interpretation, the Jews symbolize the 'psychics' who are capable of receiving enlightenment and joining the Gentiles or 'pneumatics', who are by nature the elect and do not need to be called. The discussion about the relation of Jews and Gentiles in the church thus becomes a discussion about bringing the psychics, by adoption, to join those who are by nature members of Christ. Pneumatics have so strong an element of divinity in them that their salvation is certain: they will rejoin the original divine wholeness from which they were separated. The psychics are those who have just enough of the divinity to make it possible, but not certain, that they will be saved.

However much they may have misrepresented Paul in the 'orthodox' view, the Gnostics did grasp the radical newness of his gospel. It is difficult to claim that for the next generation of orthodox writers, the so-called Apostolic Fathers. We have seen Acts and the Pastorals venerating Paul while taming him theologically, and 2 Peter contriving to regard him as an authority alongside the Old Testament yet as hard to understand. The Apostolic Fathers, who overlap in time with later New Testament books, but who can be regarded as roughly the next stage in Christian literature, complete this process. Some of them, particularly 1 Clement, Ignatius of Antioch, and Polycarp, show considerable knowledge of Paul's letters but little awareness of their central contentions. Far from embracing the idea of a new being brought about by God's grace, they tend to see Christianity as a new law, the performance of which is assisted by God (this assistance is what they mean by grace). Even 1 Clement, which seems to know 1 Corinthians almost by heart, talks about Rahab's being justified by faith *and hospitality* (12: 1). Perhaps Ignatius most reflects Pauline influence (see Ign. *Eph*. 5: 2 on *sarx* and *pneuma*, for instance), but he is so preoccupied with establishing the bishop's authority, with fighting heresy, and with achieving his own martyrdom, that other matters are relegated to the periphery. Dying with Christ becomes virtually identical with martyrdom (see Ign. *Rom.* 6: 3; *Eph.* 10: 3; *Smyrn.* 4: 2; *Trall.* 4: 2). Elsewhere in the literature the notion is scarcely understood at all.

There was a stronger emphasis on God's demands than on his gifts. No doubt this was partly because the writers needed to maintain high moral standards in the face of pagan immorality, and because of the break with Judaism and the consequent loss of the Torah tradition. Repentance, a notion at best peripheral for Paul, moves closer to the centre. The idea that people are oppressed by hostile powers, including the power of sin, and need liberation as much as forgiveness, is missing altogether. The thing that really differentiated the Pauline faith from Judaism is thus not fully grasped; except for the conviction that Jesus was the Messiah and God's true revelation, there is not much in the Apostolic Fathers different from a liberal Judaism. They opposed it, more as an external foe than as an alternative understanding of how and from what people are saved. There is almost no grasp of Paul's complex position regarding the Law; very few of this later generation started where Paul did, with a central devotion to the Law which thus was seen as a rival to Christ.

Of course, one factor was the Gnostic use of Paul already mentioned. This caused 'orthodox' writers to approach him in gingerly fashion and to make disproportionate use of the Pastorals which the Gnostics did not use much. Later in the second century Irenaeus of Lyons (*Adv. Haer.* IV xli 4) shows how Paul had to be defended against his 'heretical' adherents, and in the Clementine writings, which come from this time and later, Paul is regarded as the arch-enemy of the true (Jewish Christian) gospel.

The formation of the Pauline corpus

How did letters written to specific churches for particular reasons and in particular circumstances, come to be collected into a corpus and eventually regarded as scripture? Obviously, at first only the recipients of the several letters had copies. One view of what happened next is that for some time nothing did. It was only late in the first or early in the second century, perhaps after Acts began to circulate, that someone thought to collect the extant epistles and fragments in order to benefit a wider circle of readers. Many think this editor also welded fragments into new letters, especially in the cases of 2 Corinthians and Philippians. This is not inconceivable, for while papyrus is an excellent writing material, it tends to fray and fall to pieces. As a whole, this theory has the merit of explaining both why no one seems to refer to the letters until the end of the first century, and why no copies of the unreconstructed fragments survive. We have already mentioned a particular version of this theory which attempts to account for the letter to the Ephesians (see p. 133).

A different view of what happened sees some independent circulation of individual letters. Romans probably existed in more than one version: Marcion's edition stopped at the end of Chap. 14, and there is some other evidence for a fourteen-chapter version, as well as for a fifteen-chapter one, though most copies have sixteen chapters. Again, a weakness of the first theory is that it is impossible to recover the order of the letters in the supposed collection: early lists differ considerably, but surely a collection which was also the first 'publication' would have left a definite mark on the order? Moreover, some scholars doubt that any of the extant letters is composed of fragments, and think they are as Paul wrote them. It is argued, then, that after a period when the letters achieved increasing circulation individually, they were brought together into a collection. It cannot be said that either of these views is implausible, but the first has a slight edge on the second, because it accounts for the generation's silence about the letters that followed Paul's death.

8

Conclusion

Paul's version of Christianity faced opposition in the early church, and has done so sporadically ever since. There have always been those who see him as corrupting the simple message of Jesus and complicating it, by turning it into a religion of redemption or by subverting its Jewishness. We must now, therefore, look briefly at the relation of Paul's gospel to the teaching of Jesus and to some other early versions of Christianity. For an account of the *Variety and Unity in New Testament Thought* readers should consult the volume in this series with that title and for the question of how Pauline Christianity can be interpreted in modern times, the volume on *Biblical Interpretation*.

Pauline theology certainly has a different look and feel from the accounts of the life and teaching of Jesus in the Synoptic Gospels, both in overall impression and in detail. This is partly because letters tackling pastoral, theological, and ethical problems are bound to be more complex than works composed mostly of narrative and pithy sayings. The *genre* is different, but there is more to it than that. It would be as foolish to argue for no development from Jesus of Nazareth to Paul as to suppose that Paul betrays the simple gospel of Jesus.

Paul is not trying to present the story of Jesus or to transmit his teaching but to present a gospel about him. Jesus is not the messenger but the message; so much is surely evident from all that we have been considering. We saw at the end of Chapter 2, and have seen continually since, that Paul's interest is not in the Jesus-tradition (if he knew it), but in Christ as the one who brings the new being and the New Age. In his death and resurrection the old powers are overthrown, and new possibilities of life open up for those who believe in him and are in him. This was not just one more divine initiative, but the definitive and final one, final in the sense that everything that follows is its outworking. There is thus a double focus in Paul's thought: a focus on Christ as the eschatological Man, the final Adam, who is now the new power and authority in and under whom Christians exist; and a focus on the nature of the human dilemma, guilt and bondage, which is resolved in a totally new existence in Christ. Nothing could ever be the same again, and it was Paul's enormous and unique achievement to work out what this meant for the individual, the church, and the universe. Nobody else did it on the same scale, though the authors of Hebrews and the Johannine literature approach it most closely. It obviously could not have been done by Jesus himself, because the materials for it were not available until after his mission was accomplished.

There is thus a substantially different perspective between Jesus and Paul, which survives the fact that the writing of the gospels is chronologically second. There is also, however, an important continuity, which can now be outlined.

First, the teaching of Jesus about the kingdom, widely agreed to be in its main features one of the elements of the gospels least vulnerable to historical questioning, shows that for him the world was at the turn of the ages, and was either in the process of undergoing or would shortly undergo the establishment of God's New Age. The Markan summary of the teaching of Jesus (1: 15) catches this exactly: '"The time is fulfilled, and the kingdom of God is at hand: repent, and believe in the gospel."' Of course the use of 'gospel' indicates that Mark himself made the summary, so that this is not in so many words what Jesus went about saying, but rather gives the drift of his message. Now this identification of the present as the eschatological moment was agreed between Paul and Jesus, and indeed is Paul's point of departure.

Secondly, the kingdom proclaimed by Jesus is God's new dominion, replacing the powers under which humanity has hitherto been enslaved. The early chapters of Mark reflect this vividly. So, when Paul sees Christ as the power under and by whom Christians live, he is in continuity with the claim that in the activity of Jesus the power of God is at work (see for example Mark 3: 21–7; Matt. 12: 24–9; Luke 11: 15–22).

Thirdly, both Paul and Jesus proclaim God's acceptance of the unacceptable, the ungodly, the publicans and sinners. Paul's formulation of justification by faith is affected by his need to include a reference to the cross, but fundamentally it is in direct line with the picture of Jesus in the gospels: see for example how the parables of lost sheep, lost coin, and lost son in Luke 15 follow on the accusation in v. 1 that Jesus received sinners and ate with them. The Jesus who had fellowship with the unworthy without first requiring repentance and amendment of life has become the Christ who, according to Paul, conveys acceptance with God to those who whether Jews or Gentiles (Rom. 3: 10–31) rely on faith alone. Once again there is continuity between Paul and what is widely taken to be an authentic element in the gospel tradition.

Fourthly, for both Paul and Jesus the Law's requirements were expendable when salvation was at stake. Neither opposed the Law out of antinomianism, but both proclaimed or took for granted an even greater authority. The similarity must not be exaggerated: although Jesus is shown relegating the Sabbath law in importance, and the law about clean and unclean foods, there is no suggestion that he made the criticism in principle we find in Paul, or saw it as among the powers of the Old Age. Yet there is a distinct line of continuity between them, and both were regarded as dangerous liberals by many devout Jews.

In important respects, therefore, it is incorrect to suppose that Paul distorted the religion of Jesus. Although he begins post-Easter, and puts the person of Christ himself in the centre, the line of development is patent. Certainly his approach is more intellectual and more investigatory than any other in the New Testament. He himself was aware (see Gal. 1–2) that not all Christians accepted his version of the gospel, especially in the matter of Law-observance, but the element of argumentation rather than sheer denunciation in his letters shows that a variety of positions could be held in this and many other issues without people excommunicating each other.

His Christianity did not venerate Jesus as the great teacher, unlike Matthew's, or make much of Jesus the healer, unlike Mark's and Luke's. Its attitude to the New Age as already present is more cautious than John's, and he is not much interested in Jesus as the fulfilment of the institution and ritual of the Temple, unlike the author of Hebrews. In the most controversial area, the relation of Christians to Judaism and the Law, he is not like the Gnostic radicals who rejected the Creator God, and therefore the God of Israel, as irrelevant or malign (see 1 Cor. 6: 12ff; 10: 1ff). On the other hand he could not have agreed with Matthew that the Law stands, even if it is essentially constituted by the love commandment (cf. Matt. 5: 17–20, 43–8; 22: 34–40; 23: 3), nor with the letter of James that one is justified by works and not by faith alone (Jas. 2: 24).

Although he claimed a special revelation as the source of his version of Christianity, particularly his view of the Law, he may not have been entirely without predecessors. It is possible that in the 'Hellenists' of Acts 6 we have a group of Christians who accepted a universal mission with a relative lack of commitment to Law and Temple (so at least Acts 6:11,13f). This might explain why they were expelled from Jerusalem while the Twelve were not (Acts 8:1). Too much radicalism has probably been read into the position of Stephen and the others, of whose real views we in fact know extremely little. Nevertheless it remains possible that even before Paul there was more than one opinion in the church about the necessity of obedience to the Torah and the whole Torah.

Paul did not regard with equanimity this threat to unity. This is seen strikingly in the matter of the collection, the *koinōnia*, with which he was much occupied at the end of his ministry. We saw in Chapter 6 that this was in part those with better material resources helping the poor, but there was more to it than that. Anyone could have taken it to Jerusalem, but it was so important to him that he ran great risks in order to deliver it in person. Theologically, it expressed the unity of the church, Gentile and Jewish, and presumably this is why he is not altogether sure that it will prove acceptable (Rom. 15: 31). It may fail as an ecumenical gesture.

There may be a further reason for his running the risk of taking it himself together with representatives from the Gentile churches (see 1 Cor. 16: 3f; 2 Cor. 8: 16–24). The arrival of the Gentiles with gifts at Jerusalem was a sign of the Last Days (see Isa. 2: 2f; Mic. 4: 1f; also Isa. 60: 5f) and thus a demonstration of the hope expressed in Rom. 11 that the ingathering of the Gentiles would lead to that of the Jews, and not the reverse, as in the traditional expectation.

Whether or not the collection succeeded in its purpose, the diversity within early Christianity continued for a long time. For some centuries, as we note from the Clementine writings, there were those who saw Paul as the betrayer of the true Jewish Christian faith. Perhaps the decline in understanding him in the second century was inevitable once the church had to settle down in a world which did not end. Perhaps the whole structure of his thought was impossible to maintain once it was no longer easy to think of Christians as living on the edge of the times. Yet he has continued, even if with interruptions, to exercise a strong and creative influence on those who take Jesus Christ seriously, and to fascinate even many who do not share his faith.

BIBLIOGRAPHY

Books of General Usefulness

J. C. Beker, *Paul the Apostle. The Triumph of God in Life and Thought*, Philadelphia and Edinburgh 1980. Stress is laid on Paul's apocalyptic framework.

E. Best, *Paul and His Converts*, Edinburgh 1988. Paul's role as a pastor is important for understanding what he writes.

G. Bornkamm, *Paul*, New York and London 1971

F. F. Bruce, *Paul: Apostle of the Free Spirit*, Exeter 1977

R. Bultmann, *Theology of the New Testament*, Vol. I, London 1952. In need of correction at many points but still enormously stimulating.

W. D. Davies, *Paul and Rabbinic Judaism*, London 1970. The classical study of Paul against his Jewish background.

J. A. Fitzmyer, *Paul and His Theology*, Englewood Cliffs 1987. A revised and expanded version of *Pauline Theology. A Brief Sketch*, 1967.

M. D. Hooker, *Pauline Pieces*, London 1979 (*Preface to Paul* in the U.S.)

M. D. Hooker, *Continuity and Discontinuity*, London 1986. A highly readable exposition of Paul's relation to his native Judaism.

R. Jewett, *Paul's Anthropological Terms*, Leiden 1971. A massive study of terms like 'body', 'flesh', and 'spirit'.

W. G. Kümmel, *Introduction to the New Testament*, London 1975. Probably the best available account of such matters as authorship and date.

J. Munck, *Paul and the Salvation of Mankind*, London 1959

C. J. Roetzel, *The Letters of Paul*, Atlanta 1975, London 1983. A most useful introduction.

E. P. Sanders, *Paul and Palestinian Judaism*, London 1977. A major attack on much traditional talk about Paul in relation to Judaism; invaluable.

H. J. Schoeps, *Paul*, London 1961. A lively account by a Jewish scholar.

A. Schweitzer, *The Mysticism of Paul the Apostle*, London 1931. Despite some important idiosyncracies, this is still a basic work.

K. Stendahl, *Paul Among Jews and Gentiles*, London 1977. Polemical and lively.

D. E. H. Whiteley, *The Theology of St. Paul*, Oxford 1974. A standard work.

For many topics, the reader is well advised to consult the appropriate entries in *Theological Dictionary of the New Testament*, eds. G. Kittel and G. Friedrich, tr. G. W. Bromiley, 10 vols., Grand Rapids 1964-76, and in *The Interpreter's Dictionary of the Bible*, especially the *Supplementary Volume*, Nashville 1976.

In recent years, much work has been done on Paul from a sociological perspective. Especially recommended are:

M. Y. MacDonald, *The Pauline Churches*, Cambridge 1988

W. A. Meeks, *The First Urban Christians*, Yale 1983

G. Theissen, *The Social Setting of Pauline Christianity*, Philadelphia and Edinburgh, 1982

F. Watson, *Paul, Judaism and the Gentiles*, Cambridge 1986

Commentaries

The following are particularly valuable:

On the Greek text of Romans, J. D. G. Dunn, *Romans 1-8* and *Romans 9-16*, Word Biblical Commentary, Dallas 1988

On the English text of Romans,

C. K. Barrett, *The Epistle to the Romans*, London and New York 1957

C. H. Dodd, *The Epistle of Paul to the Romans*, London 1932

E. Käsemann, *Commentary on Romans*, Grand Rapids and London 1980

J. A. Ziesler, *Romans*, London and Philadelphia 1989

On the Greek text of 1 Corinthians, H. Conzelmann, *1 Corinthians*, Philadelphia 1975

On the English Text of 1 Corinthians,

C. K. Barrett, *The First Epistle to the Corinthians*, London and N.Y. 1968

J. Ruef, *Paul's First Letter to Corinth*, Harmondsworth 1971

On the English text of 2 Corinthians, C.K. Barrett, *The Second Epistle to the Corinthians*, London 1973

On the Greek text of Galatians,

H. D. Betz, *Galatians*, Philadelphia 1979

F. F. Bruce, *The Epistle to the Galatians*, Exeter 1982. Not a commentary, but the best recent study of the letter and packed with excellent exegesis, is J. M. G. Barclay, *Obeying the Truth*, Edinburgh 1988.

On the English text of Philippians,

R. P. Martin, *Philippians*, London 1976

J.-F. Collange, *The Epistle of Saint Paul to the Philippians*, London 1979

On the English text of Ephesians, and the other 'captivity epistles',

G. B. Caird, *Paul's Letters from Prison*, Oxford 1976

J. L. Houlden, *Paul's Letters from Prison*, London 1970

On the Greek text of Colossians, E. Lohse, *Colossians*, Philadelphia 1971

On the English text of Colossians,

R. P. Martin, *Colossians and Philemon*, London 1974

E. Schweizer, *The Letter to the Colossians*, Philadelphia and London 1982

On the English text of the Thessalonian letters,

E. Best, *The First and Second Epistles to the Thessalonians*, London 1972

On the Greek text of the Pastoral Epistles,

M. Dibelius and H. Conzelmann, *The Pastoral Epistles*, Philadelphia 1972

On the English text of the Pastoral Epistles,

J. L. Houlden, *The Pastoral Epistles*, London and Philadelphia, [2]1989

R. J. Karris, *The Pastoral Epistles*, Wilmington Del., [2]1984

On the Acts of the Apostles, E. Haenchen, *The Acts of the Apostles*, Oxford 1971

Additional Suggestions for Reading, Chapter by Chapter

Chap. 1: W. G. Doty, *Letters in Primitive Christianity*, Philadelphia 1973
R. Jewett, *Dating Paul's life (A Chronology of Paul's Life in the U.S.)*, London and Philadelphia 1979
G. Lüdemann, *Paul, Apostle to the Gentiles*, London & Philadelphia 1984

Chap. 2: D. L. Dungan, *The Sayings of Jesus in the Churches of Paul*, Philadelphia 1971
M. Hengel, *Judaism and Hellenism*, 2 vols., London 1974
E. Lohse, *The New Testament Environment*, London and Nashville 1976. Generally invaluable, but readers should be warned that what is said about Judaism (pp. 184ff) is now

seen as contentious in the light of E. P. Sanders, *Paul and Palestinian Judaism*.

A. J. M. Wedderburn, *Baptism and Resurrection*, Tübingen 1987

Chap. 3: L. Cerfaux, *Christ in the Theology of St. Paul*, Edinburgh, London, and New York, 1959

J. D. G. Dunn, *Christology in the Making*, London 1980 (also for Chap. 4)

Chap. 4: R. Banks, *Paul's Idea of Community*, Exeter 1980

B. J. Byrne, '*Sons of God'—'Seed of Abraham'*, Rome 1979

C. F. D. Moule, *The Origin of Christology*, Cambridge 1977, Chap 2

J. Rogerson, 'The Hebrew Conception of Corporate Personality: A Re-Examination', *Journal of Theological Studies* xxi (1970), 1-16

R. Scroggs, *The Last Adam*, Oxford and Philadelphia 1966

Chap. 5: articles in *Theological Dictionary of the New Testament*

M. Hengel, *The Atonement*, London 1981

R. C. Tannehill, *Dying and Rising with Christ*, Berlin 1967

J. A. Ziesler, *The Meaning of Righteousness in Paul*, Cambridge 1972

Chap. 6: N. A. Dahl, *Studies in Paul*, Minneapolis 1977, Chap. VII and pp. 9-16

J. W. Drane, *Paul: Libertine or Legalist?* London 1975

V. P. Furnish, *The Moral Teaching of Paul*, Nashville 1979

H. Hübner, *Law in Paul's Thought*, Edinburgh 1981

H. Räisänen, *Paul and the Law*, Tübingen 1983

E. P. Sanders, *Paul, the Law and the Jewish People*, Philadelphia 1983 and London 1985

G. Theissen, *Psychological Aspects of Pauline Theology*, Edinburgh 1987. Part of the book is a new look at Rom. 7.

S. Westerholm, *Israel's Law and the Church's Faith*, Grand Rapids, 1988

Chap. 7: see the commentaries and books on New Testament Introduction, plus:

C. K. Barrett, 'Pauline Controversies in the Post-Pauline Period', *New Testament Studies* 20 (1974), 229–45

E. Pagels, *Paul the Gnostic: Gnostic Exegesis of the Pauline Letters*, Philadelphia 1975

Chap. 8: R. Bultmann, 'Jesus and Paul' in *Existence and Faith*, London 1964

V. P. Furnish, 'The Jesus-Paul Debate: From Baur to Bultmann', *Bulletin of the John Rylands Library* 47 (1964–5), 342-81

K. F. Nickle, *The Collection*, London 1966

INDEX OF PASSAGES CITED

GENERAL INDEX

164